Secrets of a

Fashion Therapist

Secrets of a Fashion Therapist

What You Can Learn Behind the Dressing Room Door

BY BETTY HALBREICH

WITH SALLY WADYKA

ILLUSTRATIONS BY JEFFREY FULVIMARI

FOR ART DEPARTMENT

Cliff Street Books

An Imprint of HarperCollinsPublishers

HarperCollins books may be purchased for educational, business, or sales promotional use. For information please write: Special Markets Department, HarperCollins Publishers, Inc., 10 East 53rd Street, New York, NY 10022.

FIRST EDITION

Designed by Robbin Gourley

Library of Congress Cataloging-in-Publication Data

Halbreich, Betty.
   Secrets of a fashion therapist / Betty Halbreich with Sally
Wadyka. — 1st ed.
     p. cm.
   ISBN 0-06-270187-8
   1. Clothing and dress. 2. Fashion.   I. Wadyka, Sally.
II. Title.
TT507.H15   1997
646' .34—dc21   97-15431

97 98 99 00 01 ❖/RRD 10 9 8 7 6 5 4 3

TO MY MOTHER, CAROL STOLL—
one of the original taste makers

Acknowledgments

FROM BETTY:

All my thanks to Kathy and John, always asking, "Is it done yet, Mom?" To Greg Mills for tremendous support and Bruce Gregga for telephone calls of encouragement. To Patricia for her saintly patience and Philip, who believed in me! Jim, for his patience and then some. And to Sally— who became like a daughter and read me like a book!

FROM SALLY:

Many thanks to Patricia van der Leun and, of course, to Betty for letting me in on what has been a totally delightful collaboration. I've never spent so much time surrounded by clothes . . . and I've never been happier! To Steven and Mom and Dad for help, both legal and otherwise. And to all my friends who listened—patiently— to my daily word-count tallies and were always available to help me procrastinate at a moment's notice, you have my deepest thanks.

Table of Contents

Foreword

*B*etty Halbreich's working
endeavor, in reality, is the
same as mine—suggesting,
proposing . . . sometimes pleading, for
clothes that make people feel even better
about themselves, an elevation of sorts.
Hers is the last link to that moment of
truth! She enriches our lives. She is like
good clothes . . . a remembrance
of things that last.
That is Betty Halbreich.

—GEOFFREY BEENE

Secrets of a Fashion Therapist

...to that different drummer in all of us...

Chapter 1

GOING SHOPPING FOR THE TRUTH

Part 1

PLAYING DRESS-UP

When the snow was still up over my head in our hometown of Chicago, my mother would appear in a hat made of cherries. From the neck down she'd be in her winter fur coat, but her head would be like a harbinger of spring. And in the fall, it was the same thing: Before the leaves had even begun to turn, out would come the first felt hat of the season, always with a feather. I remember getting in the car with her and watching her fight with that hat—the feather was so long she actually couldn't get it into the car! That was just her way of announcing the change of seasons. My mother was known all over town for her style and her wit—not to mention her crazy hats. Of course, it would be hard *not* to be known around town when you're wearing flowers on your head in the middle of a Chicago snowstorm.

Thinking back, it's little wonder I ended up where I am now. My fashion education started in her bedroom when I was just a little girl. I'd sit mesmerized, watching her get dressed in sequined dresses, fox-trimmed suits, a cocktail dress with feathers lining the hem. One Christmas the photographer Victor Skrebneski gave my mother a white marabou jacket. Not many women could get away with wearing something so outrageous, but she wore that jacket to death—trailing feathers all the way. My mother has the best taste of any human being I've ever met, so who could blame me for trying to keep up? I think I started dressing up in my mother's clothes from the day I knew how to dress myself. The minute she left to go out for the evening, I'd slip into her closet and drape myself with her most lavish velvet negligées, high heels, and dazzling jewelry.

As a child, I loved playing dress-up more than anything. And in a sense, that's what I'm still doing today. Only now, instead of my mother's closet, I have all of Bergdorf Goodman to play with—seven floors filled with designer collections, glamorous evening gowns, and unique accessories. And instead of just dressing myself (or my little dolls), I now outfit some of the most beautiful and famous women in the world. And just as I never got bored in my mother's closet, the daily challenges of dressing all sizes, shapes, and types of women still gives me a little thrill. When I find just the right dress for the mother of the bride, create a movie character's entire wardrobe, or calm a nervous young woman before her first job interview (while dressing her in a knock-'em-dead new suit), I can shut my dressing room door at the end of the day and call it a success.

My mother always claimed that I walked to a different drummer when it came to dressing. Whatever my peers were doing, I deliberately went the other way. Even at summer camp, when we all had to wear a uniform, I'd find a way to put my own stamp on it. I cuffed the shorts, rolled my sleeves a certain way, tied a sweater around my neck. I'm not saying I always looked great. Maybe I even looked ridiculous at times, but that is exactly what's so much fun about fashion: taking a style risk here and there just to see what happens.

Sometimes it doesn't work at all, but then you know not to do it again, and eventually you build confidence in your ability to make smart fashion choices. That's the real secret to dressing well: It's all about attitude. The attitude of the clothes, but also what's in your head. It's about walking into a room, knowing that you look and feel good, and projecting that attitude out to everyone who sees you.

When I first started my career as a fashion consultant in

playing dress-up

1976, the phrase "personal shopper" didn't exist yet. But the customers were desperate for help. Bergdorf Goodman, which has always been New York City's most chic department store, had just about everything anyone could possibly want, but the women who ventured through the revolving doors on Fifth Avenue were often intimidated, overwhelmed, or too frightened to try anything new.

That's where I came in. From the beginning I think people came to me for reassurance and for an objective eye. When one of my customers puts something on, instead of looking in the mirror, she looks at me. I was born with a good eye, I admit. And it's a blessing. I can't deny that there is something intuitive about dressing well and knowing what works and what doesn't. But that doesn't mean you can't learn to do it yourself. It just takes a little practice and a *lot* of looking in the mirror.

I have customers who have been coming to me since the day I first opened my dressing room door. Over the years, they've brought in their friends, their mothers, their daughters, and even their granddaughters. When I first worked with Betty Buckley (who has been a customer for twenty years), she was on Broadway in *Cats*. And she's called me before every audition since then. By now, I think it's almost a superstition. I find her an outfit, she gets the part. Some of my customers think I perform miracles. I think I'm just honest. A woman who steps into my dressing room is more likely to hear "Take it off, that looks awful" than "Oooh, that's *fabulous!*"

Most days my office bears more resemblance to a three-ring circus than it does to a chic fashion show. There's a constant parade of women in all shapes and sizes: actresses, powerful executives, society types, housewives, young mothers,

I was being considered for a film based on a novel that I had tracked for three years. It was finally being produced by a great director and the cameo role I sought was really based on "the look." I called Betty, we went right to Bergdorf's, and she found me the perfect suit. I walked into the director's office in my new Calvin Klein suit and the part was mine. Only last week I called her about another film—I told Betty over the telephone the character profile—and she immediately sent me a couple of outfits, with shoes to match. Of course, I got the part. Betty is my Athena, and her art makes me feel like a goddess. Long may she reign!
—Betty Buckley, actress

and regular working women. But regardless of who they are and how much they have to spend, in the end, they keep coming in because shopping and dressing is about much more than clothes. It's something you do to make yourself feel good. It should be fun. And sometimes even funny. Because if you aren't enjoying your clothes, then you really are missing the point. I always maintain that no one walks into my office—or into any store anywhere—unless she is ready for a bit of a change. I have yet to meet a woman who can walk past a store without her nose pressed to the glass. She's desperate just to pass through. Show me a person who doesn't like new things—whether it is a frivolous adornment or a necessity—and I say she isn't a woman!

OUT OF THE CLOSET

*T*here are two things that nobody wants to face: their closet and their mirror. Most people open the closet door, then immediately shut it again—and run for cover! They can't face what they see in that closet. They hate the disorganization and the lack of continuity they find behind those closed doors. It's no wonder that the most common words women utter are: "I don't have anything to wear." Well, of course you think there is nothing to wear, because with everything in such a state of disarray, with most of the good stuff hiding behind mounds of junk, you wouldn't be able to find something to wear even if you *did* own it.

Now like it or not, I can't let you rush off to the store in an I've-got-to-buy-something frenzy until you've faced down those two nemeses: the closet and the mirror. First, the closet. Chances are, it's so packed with junk and so poorly organized

> Betty knows exactly what a client's wardrobe needs before the client even knows she needs it!
> —Susan Lucci, actress, *All My Children*

that even though you're convinced you have nothing to wear, you're equally convinced that there is not a speck of room in there for anything new. There is a simple, if rather unpleasant, solution: Bite the bullet and clean out the closet. Once you weed out what you no longer want or need, once you see some spaces start to show up between the hangers, you'll be much happier. There's no question about it. But the real challenge of a closet clean-up is deciding what stays and what goes. Now I know this is a cliché, but it really does hold true in most cases: If you haven't worn it in a year, it should be tossed. (Not literally thrown out, of course; find a needy person or a charity that accepts clothing donations.) I say get rid of things you don't wear because they don't get any younger. And if you are planning to wait around until it's retro, you're going to have a long wait. Besides, even with all the retro fashions designers are bringing back these days, the updated versions are always a little different. The same exact thing doesn't really come around again—and even if it did, would you want or be able to get back into it? When I look at the young women wearing some of the hideous polyester clothes from the seventies that they've pulled out of the back of their closets or rooted out of some vintage store, I can't help but think that anyone who was old enough to wear them the first time around is not going to be in a rush to wear those things again!

"I tossed WHAT out?"

The exception in all this tossing-out frenzy are the clothes you've really invested in. But just because you spent a lot of money on something and don't want to get rid of it doesn't mean it has to hang front and center in your closet if you aren't currently wearing it. I think the best thing to do is take the clothes you really feel indebted to, the ones you can't bear to part with yet don't wear, and put them in a separate place. A whole separate closet if you have it, or even just a corner of your closet or dresser. Think carefully before tossing out things of value. I do have things I regret getting rid of. I often ask myself, What was I thinking throwing away perfectly good alligator handbags? They would cost an absolute fortune to replace today. So, yes, sometimes it does make sense to hold on

the Closet

to a few prized possessions. Even if they *never* come back in fashion, chances are, you'll be glad to visit them every now and again.

Now I'm afraid it is time to face the mirror. You need to strip down to nothing and stand naked in front of a full-length mirror if you really want to check yourself out with an objective eye. Turn to the mirror (gulp!), and say "Here I am." It's the hardest thing to do, and it's also one of the most embarrassing things in the world. I find it very hard to do (that's why for years I didn't even *own* a mirror except the one over the sink in the bathroom!), but you really should try to analyze yourself, your assets and your flaws, while standing there with nothing on. If you can't face yourself nude, I'll give you a break: Keep just your underwear on. Either way, it takes a strong woman to really look objectively at what's reflected there.

Before you cover your eyes and turn away from that mirror, remember to look behind you as well. We are not one-dimensional, so everything you put on your body needs to be seen from every angle. Just because *you* don't often see the back of yourself, don't forget that all day long the people around you see you from every imaginable angle. When I walk to work in the mornings, I see the whole world from behind. And what a world it is back there! I see pants that are too tight, shoes that are run down at the heels, hair that's unbrushed, extremely obvious panties and/or bras showing through the clothing . . . the list goes on. Do yourself—and everyone around you—a favor and at least try to glance over your shoulder at the mirror before you rush out the door with a label sticking out of your dress, a stain on the seat of your pants, or some other disaster lurking back there.

It's easy for me to look at my customers objectively. I see

Closet Cleanup Checklist

• Look for the things you have a tendency to overdose on: Do you have six red sweaters? Five black jackets? Four navy skirts? You don't necessarily have to get rid of any of them (they're all *completely* different, right?), but just remember how many you've got the next time you're in a store and find yourself heading to the cashier with yet another red sweater, black jacket, navy skirt, or (fill in the blank with whatever you tend to collect).

• Do force yourself to get rid of clothes that *really* don't fit you anymore. There's no worse torture than keeping a closet full of gorgeous clothes you haven't been able to squeeze into in at least a decade. Let's face it: By the time you theoretically lose those five (or ten or however many) pounds, those clothes will be hopelessly out-of-date.

• Before you toss worn-out clothes and shoes in the trash, check to see if they can be fixed. Shoes are easily (and not that

→

11

expensively) revitalized—with new heels, new soles, and a good polishing, many pairs can look brand-new again. As for clothes, a good tailor or seamstress can often repair damaged knits, replace lost buttons or trim, or even revamp an outdated piece with alterations.

• Whatever can't be fixed—fabrics worn shiny from wear and cleaning, suede or canvas shoes that are irreparable, clothing with permanent stains—should definitely be tossed.

• Thrift or consignment shops are great places to dispose of what you no longer want—especially expensive "mistakes"—without the guilt. You can get cash (if it's a consignment shop) or use your donation as a charitable tax deduction.

• Organize a "swap party" with your friends. Have everyone bring clothes they no longer want and then trade with each other. Forget that you're getting it for free, and be careful not to just grab anything (which will end up in next year's discard pile). But often, one woman's trash truly is another woman's treasure!

nothing more than exactly what's in front of my eyes. A form that needs to be dressed: a head, two arms, two legs, hips, a waistline. I see that form, and I immediately think about what clothes to put on it in order to make it look its best. Go back to the mirror and try to see yourself that way. Don't let your eyes immediately fall to your hips, then scream and run for your robe. Really look at both your good spots and your bad ones without passing judgment. Now keep that image and knowledge of your body in mind and put on your favorite outfit—the one you always look and feel good in no matter what. Turn to the mirror again. Do you still like what you see? Why? Try to analyze, *objectively,* why this particular outfit makes you look good. Does the cut de-emphasize certain parts and enhance others? Is it the way the color warms up your complexion so that you suddenly look as if you've put on some makeup? Is it an eclectic mix of prints that makes you feel stylishly adventuresome? Think about all the reasons why the outfit works and file away that knowledge. It will come in very handy once you're ready to hit the stores.

I've always believed that when it comes to your wardrobe, less really is more. So don't think that just because you've now weeded all the junk out of your closet that you have to shop and shop and shop until you've stuffed it full again. I tell all my customers, "I'm not a closet dresser." And it's true. I am not here to dress their closets. I'm here to help them find clothes that are going to actually spend more time on their bodies than they do on hangers. What happens when you go shopping just for the sake of having something new is that you end up with a wardrobe full of pieces that don't work together. It's like a patchwork quilt! You walk through the store and your eye catches a piece here or there and you leave the store carrying several bags of nothing. Expensive bits of nothing.

So before you even think about going shopping, you
should think about what it is you're shopping for. Rushing out
the door with nothing but a credit card and a vague desire for
something new to wear is what gets us in trouble. Most of the
women who come to me come for a reason. They need a dress
for a wedding, a suit for an interview, casual clothes to take on
vacation. If someone comes in claiming they want to buy an
entire new wardrobe, I don't let them. I'll help them find a few
basics to start with and then I tell them to take those home and
get used to them. See how you like the styles and colors. See
how the pieces work with what's already in the closet. And the
same rule should apply to everyone. Don't try to buy a
complete wardrobe in an afternoon. Make a list of a few things
you really need and shop just for those. Remember, it's *you*, not
your closet, that should be well dressed.

Part 3

OVERCOMING CLOTHES-A-PHOBIA

Having had my fashion sense formed in Catholic boarding schools, I was drawn to red plaid, blue serge, and blazers with replicas of thorns and bleeding hearts on the pockets. Betty took this information and found a happy medium: a midnight blue velvet Valentino gown with long sleeves and a skirt to the floor. Next time she put me in gold lamé with a reptilian cast that was slinky and gorgeous. Now I go visit Betty and just buy whatever she's wearing!
—Jane Curtin, actress

*I*magine that you are about to walk through the revolving door of an enormous department store. What do you feel? Are you exhilarated by the thought of the possibilities waiting on every floor? Intimidated by the salespeople and the price tags? Overwhelmed by the vast array of clothing choices? Or maybe a little of each. Well, you're not alone. It's no wonder personal shopping has experienced such a boom in recent years. Women today need help. They are too busy or too afraid or too confused to make the right fashion choices on their own. But you don't have to be. You *can* do it alone, and do it successfully.

Think back to that little exercise in front of the mirror. Is the way you looked in your favorite outfit your ideal vision of yourself? If not, try to imagine what that ideal would look like.

(Confine your fantasies to visions that work with the body you currently have, please! We're looking for objectivity, not a wish list for the plastic surgeon.) Because before you can go shopping for a new you—or even a new sweater—you need to have an idea of what you want to look like. You must define your look. Now that self-image doesn't have to be as rigid as it sounds. You can step away and get a little more adventurous, or go back the other way and become more conservative, but underneath it all should be a solid definition of how you want to look. It's that knowledge that will give you the security to make wise fashion choices. Unfortunately it takes more than just buying a new dress to make you suddenly feel secure. Security comes with the passage of a great deal of time—and

the love of clothes

the acquisition of a great deal of self-knowledge.

Let me give you an example of a woman who came to me recently, a woman who is very conservative in her taste. I showed her a somewhat outrageous jacket designed by Yamamoto, and she practically screamed, "Betty, I'll never wear that." So I took it away. But as I did, I told her that if she kept coming to me I'd have her wearing something like that by next year. Her response: "You're probably right, but I just can't do it now." Why? Because she was afraid, and she wasn't ready to take a risk. But once you attain a certain level of security, you'll be able to make a small leap—maybe try a new jacket style, a bolder color, or a different skirt length. Think of each move as a baby step toward a more adventurous way of dressing.

In your previous attempts to go out on a fashion limb, you've probably made your fair share of mistakes (and they most likely ended up in your discard pile during the closet cleanup). Consider those missteps as part of your learning process. I've gotten to the point where I can actually walk into a store, buy a jacket without even trying it on, and know that it'll fit perfectly and look right on me. The only way to educate yourself to that point is through trial and error. If you can't look at six different style jackets and immediately know which one best suits your figure, then go try on all six and analyze yourself in the fitting room mirror. Take advantage of the three-way vantage point to check for the way it falls over your hips, how it stretches across your shoulders, or to see if it rides up in the back. This is your education in getting to know your body and what looks good on it. We all know that the same body can look entirely different depending on what it's wearing. It's your job to learn the difference between the dress that makes you look like a million bucks and the one that'll make you look like you're wearing a burlap sack.

Flipping through magazines is one way of educating yourself because they do predict the future of fashion and show you—on some level—what you might expect to find in the stores in the coming season. But do many of us really see ourselves and our lives and taste reflected on those glossy pages? Not at all! So don't look to the fashion magazines as a bible on how to dress; look to them merely to glean *ideas* of what you might like to wear. Often you may find that what's reflected in the magazines and what's available at your favorite store are two completely different things. That said, you can still take the knowledge you learned from the pages of *Vogue*— that pants are slimmer this season or that brown is *the* color to wear—and shop according to your own taste, price level, and fashion sense.

There *are* some rules when it comes to dressing with style. And by the end of this book, I will have taught them all to you, and, perhaps more importantly, given you the permission to break them. Because great style shouldn't be formulaic and rigid. It should be as eclectic and edgy as you want it to be. So take whatever rules,

Clones

tips, and secrets you glean over the next several pages, park them somewhere in the back of your brain, and then as soon as you've gained the confidence to shop anywhere and do it with flair, feel free to discard those rules. After all, fashion is really nothing to be feared.

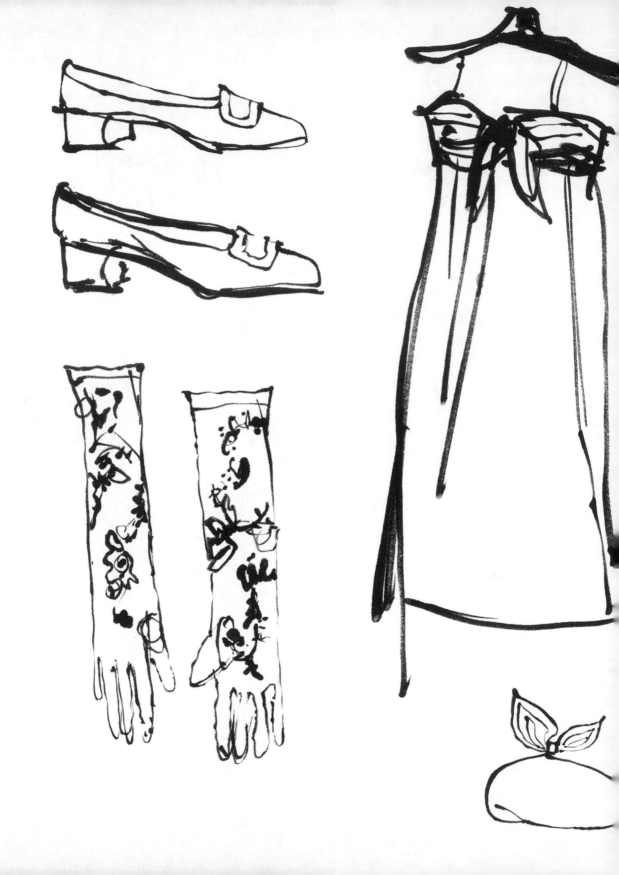

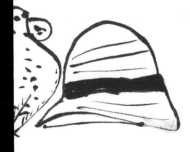

Chapte

WARDRO
AREN'
BUILT I
DAY

Part

1

STARTING FROM SCRATCH

I like to think of buying clothes and building a wardrobe the same way I think about decorating a house. Neither activity should be wrapped up in a single, marathonlike shopping spree, and neither should ever be considered "done." In your home, you want to continue all your life to amass things around you that you love. Things that make you happy. And your wardrobe should be the same way. It should keep evolving for years so that at any given time your closet holds something new as well as a few things you've had (and loved) for years. Think of building your wardrobe as an ongoing project—not a chore, but a carefully calculated labor of love. It's all about the love of clothes and beautiful things that make you feel good!

Although I'm dead set against getting rid of everything you own and starting over at ground zero, there are certain key

transitional moments in a woman's life when a substantial—
and near-total—wardrobe overhaul seems in order. The first
major milestone is the transition from college or graduate
student to working woman. This is the point at which most
women really start to compile the foundations of a basic
wardrobe that—if chosen well—will evolve with them over the
next several years. Certain supertrendy items may be given away
after a season of having fun with them, but a good core
wardrobe is not a disposable thing.

To start a wardrobe from scratch is a terrifying prospect
for most women. There's fear of having to max out the charge
cards in order to buy a full closet, fear of making expensive
mistakes, and uncertainty about being locked into a certain
look. Although your fashion sense should continue to evolve
and develop all your life (just as your wardrobe does), the

question that paralyzes most of us is, Where do we begin? Fashion sense is part innate and part osmosis. You pick up a little of it every time you glance through a magazine, stroll through a store, peruse a catalog, or window-shop on your lunch hour. I can make proclamations about what to wear and what not to wear with what, but that's not going to help you develop your own personal sense of style. That's something you are going to have to do on your own.

So let's go back to the young woman with the new job and the empty closet. If you're in that position (or, similarly, if you are heading back to work after years of being a stay-at-home mom), the first step, before running out to the store, is to make a list of what you really need to get right away. I'm talking about just the absolute basics, because I strongly believe that no one should buy more than a few pieces at a time. Decide what's essential to get you ready for those first weeks on the job—and then make a separate list of things you think you'd like to add a little bit later. Next, educate yourself a bit about what's available and what's particularly hot this season. Flip through a few fashion magazines and check out the sorts of styles you feel drawn to, and even clip out a couple of pictures to give you a visual reminder of what you're looking for while you're wandering through the stores. This isn't so much an exercise in finding the *exact* pieces you want to buy, as it is to help you identify the *types* of clothing you're looking for. So just because you rip out a picture of a Gucci shift dress from *Vogue* doesn't mean you have to break the bank and buy *that* dress—or even a stitch-for-stitch knockoff. You can use the picture to give you ideas of the sort of cut you like, a length, a color, or whatever. And since money is usually a real issue for the woman just starting out, it's also a good idea, after you've made your list and looked at some pictures, to give yourself a budget. Realize that putting together a basic professional wardrobe is an investment in yourself and your career, and be willing to spend more than you did on your college clothes. This does not mean, however, that you have to go into massive debt just to get yourself dressed. Think about what's realistic in terms of your own financial situation, and impose a limit on how much you're willing to spend for each of the items on your list (and remember to consult that list whenever a pushy salesperson tries to talk you into buying a too-expensive item).

Now that you're armed and ready to brave the store, try repeating my favorite fashion mantra in your head as you move from department to department: Less is more, less is more, less is more. This is my way of keeping you from leaving the store with a dozen shopping bags full of God-knows-what, having spent your next two months' paychecks. I find that when somebody really gets it in her head to buy clothes, she generally gets overanxious and needs to stop somewhere, mid-store, to do a reality check on her shopping progress. Even if you can afford to do it, I don't recommend buying too much at once. Let's work on just the basics for now, okay?

The obvious place to begin your wardrobe is with a suit that will serve as the foundation for everything else you buy or already own. What kind of suit you should choose depends, in part, on the field you're in. Before you go investing a lot of money in pantsuits or several pairs of expensive trousers, be sure it's okay to wear them to the office. As archaic as it seems, there are still some firms where skirts remain the rule. But generally speaking, a simple (and not too trendy) suit in a dark tone is a good first-purchase bet. If you can afford to buy two suits at once, I'd recommend finding a jacket and skirt and a jacket and pants that can be mixed up and worn with each other to instantly expand your options. The next step is finding

Blending Your Basics

- Whenever you bring home a new outfit, or a couple of new pieces, don't just hang them in the closet, play with them.

- Immediately check the rack and your dresser drawers for other things to wear with them.

- Try on several different combinations before you put your new clothes away (you won't have time to do it when you're in a rush to get to work, so if you don't experiment now, you probably never will).

- Don't forget the power of simple accessories. Put a new skirt on with various colored tights or different styles of shoes (from sophisticated pumps to chunky-heeled boots).

- Think beyond the current season: Try on a new wool gabardine suit with T-shirts as well as turtlenecks.

a variety of pieces to wear under the suit—from a couple of simple, man-tailored shirts to a twin set. For warmer weather or a more casual day at the office, add a couple of plain T-shirts from the Gap. (No one needs to spend a lot of money on a designer version of the cotton tee!) And that's all I will let you buy on your first day out.

basic math :

Now go home with these ten or so pieces and lay them all out on the bed. You should begin to see the myriad outfits these few pieces can create. Don't be afraid to deconstruct the suits, and don't forget about what's already hanging in your closet—chances are, you can mix the old and new together to come up with several more looks. Put on a pair of jeans with the crewneck sweater and one of the suit jackets and then toss the cardigan around your neck. Or put on the suit trousers with a white tee and sneakers or flat sandals. Keep experimenting, and you'll find that suddenly your new work wardrobe also includes several options that will take you way beyond the office.

When you're putting together a whole wardrobe, the key is making sure it all mixes and matches. You need to pick a palette and try to work within it. For example, a woman came to me recently looking to buy a couple of suits, a dress or two, a coat, and enough tops to coordinate it all. We started by finding the coat—a burgundy quilted coat that she loved even though it was a color she thought she would never wear in a million years. (See, it does pay to just try on something new once in a while!) Next I put her in a gray flannel suit with a chocolate brown tank under it. The second suit we found was brown, and we put a very pale blue sweater under it. But the beauty of it is that the brown tank would also work under the brown suit, as would a black top she had at home. The last thing she got was a little cranberry knit dress that looked fabulous under the coat or with the gray suit jacket over it. So she ended up with a somewhat colorful wardrobe—brown, gray, and burgundy, accented with a touch of light blue—but all the pieces can be mixed together, and these few pieces became a very basic, wearable assortment.

Now for the things you may want to add as soon as you've

The Five Commandments of Building a Basic Wardrobe

- Don't try to buy it all in a lunch hour.

- No matter how "in" a certain weird color is this season, don't buy an expensive suit that shade and expect no one to notice when you wear it three times a week.

- Shoes, a handbag, and accessories are a vital part of even the most basic wardrobe (but you've got to read on to the next chapter for tips on how to pick them).

- There's a difference between investment dressing and breaking the bank. Don't buy anything that will accumulate interest on your credit card for years before you will be able to pay it off.

- Do buy the best you can reasonably afford. (Hint: Think quality. If you can afford either a really good wool sweater or a poorly made cashmere one, get the wool.)

The Coat Closet

As you think about adding to your coat collection from season to season, consider these styles as the building blocks of a complete outerwear wardrobe.

CLOTH COAT: This should be your first priority, and since it will most likely be the coat you wear most (to work over suits, dresses, or pants as well as for dressier evening occasions), invest in one that's neutral in color (black, camel, brown, gray, navy), roomy enough to fit over a suit jacket, and long enough to cover most, if not all, of your skirts and dresses.

DOWN COAT: If you live in a cold climate, you'll need a coat that's warm even in a deep freeze. The advantage of down is that it

down coat

had a chance to live with and play with the original purchases awhile (plus time to pay off the credit card bill you rang up during that initial shopping spree). For dressier work events, cocktail parties, or even just a dinner date, a simple black dress—like a sleeveless shift—may sound hopelessly clichéd, but it really is the best one-dress-does-it-all investment. Look for a dress in a lightweight wool crepe, jersey, or gabardine that you can wear virtually year round, dress up with a pearl choker, long beads, or a chiffon scarf, or dress it down with a suit jacket or cardigan. This may sound too boring, but it doesn't have to be, depending on how you wear it. And when your goal is to build a basic wardrobe, you need to be careful not to get lured by too many of-the-moment looks. On a limited budget, buying things with planned obsolescence is not a wise way to spend your money.

To keep yourself from getting too tired of your new basics, you should, however, allow yourself to add a few fun touches whenever you can afford to—whether it's some fresh color or a few trendier, but hopefully inexpensive, pieces. Now just in case you think I'm contradicting myself (because I just mentioned above that you don't want to buy a lot of faddish stuff), I'm not. I'm simply trying to teach you good clothes-buying skills that will help you shop wisely your entire life. I'm suggesting that you add some color—like a bold red (almost everyone looks great in red) or rich hunter green—in small amounts, in a sweater, a silk shell, a handbag, or a scarf. And unless your taste naturally runs to the ultraconservative, picking up on one or two trends a season and mixing them with your core wardrobe will keep you looking, and feeling, up-to-date. And by adding just a couple of trendy pieces—a pair of hip-hugger pants, something in a sleek high-tech fabric, or a different shape or length skirt—you won't be dooming yourself to a wardrobe that needs to be tossed out every year. The basic foundation can remain the same, while the fads rotate in and out with the whims of fashion and your mood.

Now if you are going on this starter shopping spree in the fall (and let's face it, fall and winter clothes really are more worthy of investment than little summer dresses), you will probably need to save some room in your budget for buying a coat. This is a big-ticket purchase, so you need to make sure you do it wisely. In keeping with the concept of investment dressing, you will want to look for a coat that is on the classic side—anything extremely trendy will look passé before you can even get it out of mothballs next season. Also, bear in mind that this is one piece of clothing you put on nearly every day for several months in a row. In other words, you'd better make sure you won't get sick of it! Think about that before you fall in love with a red-and-pink plaid duffel coat. Sure it looks like fun now, but picture yourself in mid-March slipping it on for the one hundred and tenth time and see how much you still love it! Also, think about what you will need to do in this coat. Do you drive to and from work? If so, you need a coat that allows you to get in and out of the car without getting too entangled. Do you ride a subway? Then you probably want to opt for a dark color that won't show dirt too quickly.

The good news is that we've come a long way in terms of how we think about coats. There are no longer really any hard-and-fast rules about what style of coat looks appropriate for which situation. For example, I saw a woman the other day taking her child to school. She had on a very luxurious, long mink coat over jeans, a turtleneck, and loafers. She'll wear that same easy, beautiful mink coat over an evening dress, and maybe even over a suit to go to a meeting. We can't really categorize coats anymore, and better yet, for those making a big

will keep you warm but it is very light to wear.

SHEARLING: This is a big investment, but one that will see you through years of cold winters. A coat that's a seven-eighths length (hits right above the knee) is the most versatile.

Shearling coat

PEA COAT: A perfect casual country or city coat that looks equally great over jeans and a big sweater or black tights and a miniskirt.

SWING COAT: This is a great extra coat to have—it's generally made in lighter weight materials, making it perfect for early spring or warmer climates.

LINED RAINCOAT: Probably the smartest coat investment you can make. Use the shell over your cloth coats to protect them (during a rain or snow storm), use the coat with the

→

lining for all but the coldest temperatures. If you have an old fur coat you no longer wear, have a waterproof fabric put over it to create a luxurious lined raincoat.

FUR: It's still one of the ultimate luxuries of all time. But you don't have to get a whole coat to experience a taste of it—look for a fur-trimmed cloth coat or even a fur hat or earmuffs.

fake fur
(tiger print)

fur lined

FAKE FUR: With more and more designers working in fake furs, it's becoming a good investment. It's younger and more fun than the real thing, and it goes over everything from jeans to evening wear.

DOUBLE-FACED WOOL: This is another little luxury to add to your coat collection (again, watch the sales). Whatever the style, double-faced (unlined) wool makes a wonderful soft, light coat.

investment, style and fit do not change radically every year. Of course, certain trendier coats come and go—Prada brought back the skinny, fitted coat last winter, and a few years ago chic young women were raiding thrift stores for the old fake-fur chubbies—but most simple styles, from the balmacaan to the parka, don't get dated even after a season or two.

Your basic wardrobe of coats (and it does pay to build up a collection of different styles and weights) can include several classic shapes that will take you through all sorts of weather and occasions. You really can't get by with just one coat. After all, you put one on nearly every day of your life, so you need to think about building a wardrobe of coats that covers you for all seasons, climates, and occasions. But that said, no one (regardless of the size of her wallet) is going to run out and buy four coats at once. This is one situation in which I'm a big proponent of watching the sale racks. You can usually find great coats on sale because, unlike some other pieces, they really don't look archaic by the end of the season. Buy one you like on sale, especially a fun, "extra" coat, and put it away for next year. That is not a bad investment as far as I'm concerned.

pea
coat

cloth c

WHOSE IS IT?

T he minute women are able to afford it—and often even if they can't—they become obsessed by designer labels. I can't tell you how many times a day I hand someone something to try and the first words out of her mouth are, "Whose is it?" Normally this is prefaced by a disclaimer about how she doesn't really care about the designer and doesn't usually even look, but just out of curiosity . . . Yeah right! These women are label-buyers, and it doesn't happen only at the haute-couture level. There are women who are just as addicted to the Gap or Liz Claiborne as others are to Chanel and Armani. It seems that the phrase "Whose is it?" has become a sort of shopping mantra.

I think that women look to these labels as a kind of security blanket. The Chanel suit becomes like a coat of armor—nothing can harm you (and you will never look *wrong*), so long as you have it on. Some women are so insecure about choosing clothes that they really feel they need to wear something that practically screams out "I am a designer dress!" It's a shame that so many women have allowed themselves to be such clones. I think very few women are truly eclectic in their style. There are very few Diana Vreelands out there. Vreeland was not conventionally beautiful, but she knew her body and she knew her face, and she knew how to make herself interesting looking. She constantly created an image for herself. All of today's models and actresses look exactly the same. It's an age of cloning: Too many fashionable women today all try desperately to look the same.

Why have we all gotten so brainwashed into wanting labels? The mania has gone mainstream—even small children know Calvin Klein and Tommy Hilfiger. And teenagers are as logo conscious as their parents, if not more so. Everything has a logo on it now, whether you shop at Gucci, JCPenney, or from the street vendors—and people *want* that label. It has become a way of categorizing. If you find something you like—the quality, the fit, the value—you are going to check out the name because you will want to keep going back to it. Women, quite understandably, become very loyal to name brands when it comes to fit—whether it's panty hose, bras, pants, or jackets.

There is, undoubtedly, a certain security in purchasing a "name"—whether it's Ralph Lauren, or Worthington from JCPenney. You feel you are getting a known quantity along with that label. But I think this obsession to know whose name is on every label goes beyond that. Some of it is curiosity, and the curiosity stems from the price. Let's say you find a jacket you like, then you look at the price tag and see that it's very expensive. The next thing you do—to help you decide if you think it might be worth that amount of money—is check the label to see whose it is. There's a thought process at work here: If the label says Designer X or Brand Y, you may think, Okay, I'm getting something for the money because I've heard good things about his clothes, or this is a brand I've always been pleased with. When you see a name you recognize, it also makes you feel confident that you are dressing yourself well. That's why so many designers have branched out beyond their high-priced, top-of-the-line clothing collections to put their logo or their initials onto lower-priced clothing, underwear, handbags, you name it! Because no matter what the price level, the customer still feels she has purchased some bit of cachet along with that famous name.

Besides the security, and perhaps excitement, of owning a piece of designer clothing, what are you actually getting when you invest in a big-ticket, big-name item? Sometimes, not much. I see clothes that look like junk—badly sewn seams, threads hanging everywhere, cheap fabrics—at every price level. All clothing is expensive today, and a bigger price tag doesn't

Piecing Together an Investment-Dressing Portfolio

If you're ready to move into the corner office (or at least want to look like you belong there), now is the time to add some more luxurious items to your basic wardrobe. Here are my top picks of the pieces that will give you the highest rate of return for your investment.

- **Balmacaan coat:** This single-breasted, nonbelted, man's-style coat is much more versatile than a slim reefer coat. Look for one in a luxurious cashmere or cashmere-and-wool blend, and be sure to try it on over a suit jacket, because this coat should take you to work as well as out in the evening.

- **A good suit in a dark color:** Invest in one with a single-breasted jacket because they not only look better on most women, but they aren't as trendy as some other styles. Look for a suit that's made of lightweight wool gabardine so you will be able to wear it year-round.

→

- **Suede jacket:** People are intimidated by suede (yet covet it more than anything), but if you buy an unlined suede jacket you can wear it as a shirt, a jacket, and an outerwear jacket for both work and weekends.

- **A-line raincoat:** In the winter you can layer underneath it, and in the warmer weather the lining zips out, leaving just the waterproof shell. This is truly an all-weather, all-season coat. Make sure it's long enough to wear over your longest dresses and skirts, and find one that's not belted (it will be easier to fit a jacket underneath).

- **A big sweater:** While there are trendy sweater styles that come and go, a great big sweater—in the most luxurious knit you can afford (especially cashmere)—is always a good, long-lasting investment.

always guarantee better fabric, better construction, or a better fit. If you are looking at two cotton shirts—one from the Gap, the other by Designer X—are you going to see blatant differences in quality and construction? Probably not. The designer version may be made from a finer, smoother fabric or it may have slightly better detailing (buttons, cuffs, and so on), but few people would probably be able to spot the difference once you put it on under your suit.

I think the differences are much more obvious (and, in many cases, worth paying for) when you get into clothing that's made from luxury fabrics. Yes, expensive cashmere does feel better in the hand, hold its shape better, and last longer than the cheap variety (see Chapter 6 for more on cashmere). Even some designer-level wools have a much more luxurious feel than their less expensive counterparts; for example, top-quality merino wool can feel cashmere-soft against the skin as compared to itchier wool-and-acrylic blends. And high-quality leather and suede are exquisitely supple and buttery compared to the stiffer feel of some lesser-quality skins. Your hand can feel it. Your hand can also assess the quality of suede with this simple test: Rub your hand over anything suede—gloves, a jacket, a handbag—and make sure no color residue is left behind. That's known as crocking, and it's something that will not cure itself over time. With suede, you can generally tell by the price if you're getting good quality. Stick to the well-known manufacturers, not the bargain bazaars. This is a situation where it is worth stretching your wallet open a little wider and buying the best you can possibly afford.

The other reason that fashion watchers look to what the designers are making is to pick up on the general trends and directions for the coming seasons. Out of a designer's runway show will come news of the hot shapes, colors, and fabrics for the next season. Years and years ago, the only way to get that kind of up-to-the-minute fashion was to buy the real thing, find a dressmaker who could copy the latest looks, or go to a store like the old Orbachs, which churned out line-for-line copies of the European designers' collections. These days, the big trends from the fashion shows in Milan, Paris, and New York have trickled down to the mainstream and are being sold at the Limited practically before the models step off the runway!

I think it's fantastic that you absolutely don't have to spend a fortune simply to stay in style. But that's not to say that you can't still learn from what the designers are doing. If you can't afford to treat yourself to a piece of designer clothing, then at least treat yourself to a visit to the designer floor at the department store. Don't be intimidated because you know you're not planning to buy anything. Just take a tour and really look at what's available. Touch the fabrics, check out the construction of the jackets, see what length the skirts are and which colors are being shown as accents. Now whether you go from there to the designers' bridge, or secondary, lines or to a discount store like Target to make your actual purchases, you can use this information to pick up on the season's best looks.

But here's the one thing you really have to keep in mind when shopping, and I just can't reiterate it enough: You don't need to buy seasonally anymore. I feel that very strongly. If you choose well—and it can be done at any price level—anything

- A lightweight, long-sleeved bodysuit: They come in all price levels—from the Gap to Wolford—but it's a worthwhile investment regardless of cost. A bodysuit is the perfect piece to pack for traveling, and wonderful for layering under jumpers, sweaters, a suit jacket, or wearing on its own with a pair of jeans.

- A leather handbag: While everyone may be into the nylon backpacks (like Prada), a quality leather handbag will last you a lifetime. My advice: Buy an imitation trendy backpack on the street and spend the real money on the real leather.

- A silk scarf: Hermès is the classic—and with good reason. A large silk square can change the look of an outfit faster than anything else. Collect them, experiment with them, enjoy them.

goes in fashion today. The little mandarin collar isn't out because the pointed collar is in. The pointed collar isn't out because the scoop neck is in. If you build a wardrobe of clothes that you like and that you feel are becoming on you, they won't be old hat next season—or even the season after that. And if you do get a bit tired of something in your closet, put it aside and rest it awhile. Often, when you pull it out again it will look very good; it will feel almost new to you, and you'll be excited to put it on again. And when that happens, you *know* you have made a good investment.

DRESSING THE PARTS

*A*n essential aspect of putting together a long-lasting wardrobe—one that grows and matures with you, as it were—is figuring out how to dress your body to look its best. If you don't ever figure that out, you can buy the most beautiful clothes in the world and still end up with a closet filled with pieces that you consistently put on, take one look at in the mirror, and then rip off and stuff back into the closet. I don't care if you are a size four or a size fourteen or a size twenty, every woman I know thinks she has a fit problem. I've never seen one woman who goes into the dressing room and says, "Wow, I look great! Everything always fits me so perfectly!" When it comes to women's body insecurities, I could draw you an anatomy chart and run straight through it. I hear everything from "I hate my hair" right on down past "My stomach sticks out" and "My

I have had customers from eighteen to eighty years old, from a size two to a size twenty. I have watched the same silk pants sold to one woman for a black-tie event and to another as a beach cover-up. The right person, like Betty, can help a woman see herself differently from what she has always perceived herself to be.
—Michael Kors, designer

37

"i hate my hair"

"my stomach sticks out"

"i hate my legs!"

"my hips are too wide!"

hips are too wide" to "I hate my legs." I guess what it boils down to is that we're all looking to clothes to hide our so-called problem areas and cloak our insecurities. But the way I look at it, when I dress a woman— whether she's a size twenty or a size two petite—I'm really dressing a personality. The clothes are only concealing or flattering what is underneath.

I think we're in a period of definite evolution when it comes to body shapes. At one end of the spectrum is the fact that a growing percentage of American women are seriously overweight. And at the other end are the legions of women who have taken to working out with a vengeance. They may be slim, but they're also building up broader shoulders, bigger biceps, and more muscular thighs. Unfortunately, designers aren't taking either of these factors into consideration when they cut clothes. Consequently many women are having to change sizes. And if you've been in that position, you know how hard it can be. You think you've been a perfect size eight forever and suddenly you have to take a size ten. I try to brainwash my customers to not pay any attention to whatever size the label says. It's the fit that's important. You've got to remember that only you know the size anyway. It's not like there's a big label on your back saying "size fourteen." What everyone else sees is how the clothing fits you. And believe me (and your mirror), a garment that fits you properly will flatter you much more than one that's too tight but has that coveted low-number size on the tag.

While every woman may be convinced that she's difficult

to fit, the large-size woman is the one who has the worst time finding any clothes at all. Fashion today is, admittedly, not geared to the larger woman, but there's always *something*. This customer needs to learn—just like everyone else— how to buy pieces that flatter and how to coordinate them to get more outfits for the money. And you also have to be willing to try a lot of things on. Don't get yourself into the rut of thinking that you can only wear one style of skirt or one type of dress. I bring customers things sometimes that they look at in a panic: "Oh, Betty, I can't even try that on. I know it'll look awful on me." But I can't tell you how many times, once I've convinced them to just slip it on, they fall in love with their reflections in the mirror.

There's no one magic formula for dressing that'll guarantee you a skinny new look. Part of it is definitely attitude and the confidence with which you wear clothes, because no matter what I put on a size sixteen woman, I'm never going to make her look like a size six. You need to learn to be content within your own skin and dress accordingly. Some women feel more comfortable trying to hide under loose layers, while another customer of mine (a size sixteen to eighteen) insists on having everything fitted— she tucks in all of her blouses, wears belts. And I say good for her. It's not like she's really kidding anyone either way. Whatever exists, exists. And you really have to get past what I call the "five-pound syndrome." Every day I see women squeezing themselves into too-small

Dressing in Larger Sizes: The Facts Versus the Fiction

FICTION: Wearing a jacket will make me look heavier.

FACT: A square, boxy jacket will make you look bulky, but an elongated, softly fitted shape will flatter.

FICTION: Any pair of pants will make my hips look as wide as a house.

FACT: Pants with clean lines (no pleats, no pockets) can be slimming.

FICTION: I need to wear dark colors to conceal my flaws.

FACT: Wearing black, or other dark colors, *will* make you look thinner. But wearing color—even just as an accent—will make you look prettier.

FICTION: Elastic waists are purely a last resort for when nothing else fits.

FACT: An elastic-waist skirt or pants, with a longer top worn over it, creates a svelte look because the elastic allows the fabric to

dresses claiming that they'll wear them as soon as they lose five pounds. You absolutely should not buy clothes that way. Buy clothes to flatter the body you have *now*. When you take home that "I'll lose five pounds" dress, it hangs there in the closet—price tag still attached—taunting you to fit into it. If you have gained weight (and really do plan to lose it imminently), you should still bite the bullet and buy the larger size. You can always have it taken in and adjusted to your new, thinner body once you actually have lost the weight.

When you're trying to disguise or flatter your figure, the right fabrics can be critical. I think the right fabric can make somebody look like she lost ten pounds. Heavier women (or anyone trying to conceal wide hips or a big bosom) should stay away from really stiff fabrics that make clothes look and feel overly structured. That sort of built-in shape adds bulk and emphasizes all the parts you're trying so hard to de-emphasize. Prove it to yourself by trying on a stiff organza or heavy, starched cotton skirt. Then try on a skirt in a similar shape that's made from a soft, fluid, diaphanous fabric like silk, chiffon, velvet, or lightweight wool crepe. You look much better in the second one, right? That's because what all of the softer fabrics have in common is a sense of movement. They flow around the body and cling without gripping, so they make you feel feminine and sexy. Certain shapes (especially when combined with the right fabrics) have the same effect. Any style that has a bit of swing to it is very flattering for a larger figure or a woman with wide hips—shapes like A-line dresses and swing coats. I think movement in clothes is very important. It's a very glamorous feeling to walk and feel your clothes swinging around you.

Now the large-size woman does not have the monopoly on tricks for disguising or trimming down her figure. Since I see every shape, size, and proportion of woman in my dressing room every single day, I have, over the years, come to rely on various little subterfuges that help me to flatter every flaw (even those that exist primarily in the customer's brain). It all goes back to that mirror. You really need to confront it honestly and objectively when you get dressed, but try not to get too obsessed about the image reflected there. I hear every day the litany of things women hate: their elbows, the backs of their knees, the back of their necks, their backs, the bags under their eyes, the lines around their mouths, the veins on their hands or legs, freckles . . . the list goes on and on. All I can do is try to distract them, and that's what you have to do. Distract yourself by dressing in clothes that take away from what you think of as the bad parts and accentuate the positive.

I had a customer come in the other day wearing a suit with a mandarin-collared jacket buttoned right up to the neck. She had a **large bosom**, and being all covered up like that made her appear extremely heavy. I took one look at her and thought, I'll be lucky if I find size fourteens to fit her. But the amazing thing was that, the minute she undressed, I saw that she wasn't large at all. She had a great Rubenesque figure that included a very full bosom. Depending on how she dresses, she can look either heavy and bulky or much trimmer but still curvy. I took her out of her covered-to-the-neck jacket and put her in one that was single-breasted, nipped in slightly at the waist, and had a V neck. She looked terrific. I swear it took ten pounds off her!

When you're dressing up for evening it's especially sexy to go for a low neckline. If you are uncomfortable showing a lot of cleavage, then find a top that covers your entire bustline, but no more. If you try to conceal your shape entirely, you'll make yourself look much heavier and shapeless, which is never an attractive option.

hang evenly all the way around without pulling anywhere.

FICTION: Stripes and patterns are to be avoided like the plague.

FACT: Evaluate each piece of clothing individually. Not all stripes will make you look fat, just as not all solid black dresses will make you look thin. But when all is said and done, yes, subtle vertical pinstripes will elongate you a bit (just don't expect miracles).

FICTION: The more I cover myself up, the better I'll hide my weight.

FACT: Showing a little skin is feminine and sexy on any woman. Try a V neck that reveals your cleavage or maybe a strapless dress for evening with a chiffon scarf around your neck.

The other thing the large-bosomed woman should watch out for is the dreaded gaping blouse (actually even smaller women are often guilty of this). How many times have you seen a woman with that huge gap between buttons putting her bra on display? It's absolutely tragic that women will walk around like that. You may think no one will see because you have your suit jacket on, but eventually that jacket always makes its way onto the back of the chair and there you are with your blouse open to the world! I'd rather see a woman with a blouse that was a little large all over than to see one that tugs across the chest. Please, please, please check yourself out in the mirror (from every angle) before you leave the store with a new blouse. And if it doesn't look right, don't buy it. It's certainly not going to fit better once you get it home!

I'm always amazed to see a woman who is self-conscious about her **broad shoulders.** To me this is not a figure problem—she's the problem because she's so concerned with disguising them. The obvious thing to avoid if you do have broad shoulders are shoulder pads. If your greatest fear is that you already look like a linebacker, then extra padding is going to be the last thing you want to see. Don't be afraid to rip shoulder pads out of clothing. Often they are just basted or Velcroed on anyway and can be easily removed without damaging the fabric. To give the illusion of narrowing the shoulders usually means eliminating as much of the structure as possible. Try a soft jacket or even a sweater set instead of a rigid, stiff-shouldered, structured suit jacket and you'll immediately look more feminine. And I know you probably hate wearing sleeveless garments because you think they make you look like a board, but the trick is all in the angle of the cut. For evening, instead of a high-necked, sleeveless shift, try one with straps that are cut in at an angle toward your neck, or even a halter. As soon as you expose more skin, the angled line takes away from the squareness of the shoulders.

Women with **narrow shoulders** really do have a big problem. Here you have to build up, but the key is to do it so that it still looks natural. I don't want people to look like they are walking around with the hanger still in the jacket (which is the impression some of these awful, stiff, unnatural shoulder pads give). So the trick is to adjust your proportions by increasing the shoulder, but not throw off the proportions by *over*-increasing the shoulder. When I work with narrow-shouldered customers, I rip out a lot of the oversize pads and scalp them. We'll scoop out the stuffing or slice the pad in half before sewing it back in. Or you could also replace the pads with softer muslin-covered ones that you can find at any

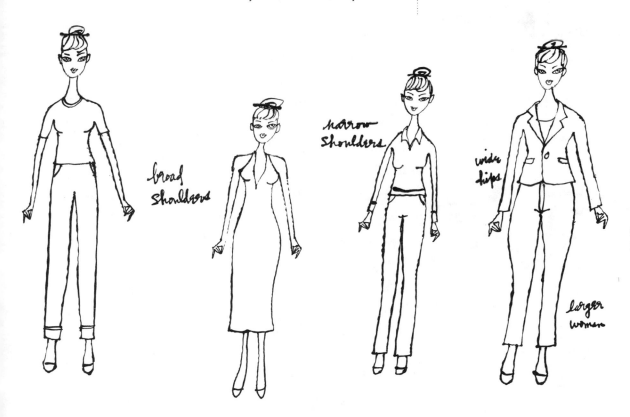

broad shoulders

narrow shoulders

wide hips

larger women

notions store. The effect will be a much more natural-looking shoulder.

My real pet peeve is these ridiculous pads that women can't seem to stop clipping onto their bra straps: They're like a security blanket. I have customers who even clip them in before putting on a T-shirt! It's hideous—worse than falsies! These pads are constantly lopping all over the place so that you end up with one shoulder up, one shoulder down, and your clothes are God knows where. It really does disfigure the clothes when you try to stick these things in everything. Whenever I have a customer who comes in with these pads I always try to hide them so she'll leave without them! If you are one of these shoulder-pad addicts, take my advice and toss the things out. Believe me, you won't miss them. And your clothes will thank you.

Now you may think that **the size four woman** doesn't have a care in the world, but if she's thin and also short, she can have a *very* hard time finding things that look right on her. I know that petite lines have made this dilemma a bit easier to work with, but even petites don't always solve every fit problem. For instance, if you're short, but long-waisted (which can happen), you'll find yourself unable to get into most petite-sized pants and even the jackets will often hit you in the wrong place. For the shorter woman, proportion is key. Everything you wear doesn't have to be short. It's a matter of objectively eyeing the proportions—you might be able to wear a longer jacket if it's paired with a short skirt or a more cropped jacket with slim trousers.

I hear so many women complain that they can't stand their backsides, but this is one complaint I refuse to take seriously. Having a nice, **full, round backside** makes your figure look young. I always say to these women, "If I'm still around twenty years from now, come back to me and we'll see if you aren't now bemoaning the fact that your backside is gone!" Because the backside does droop and flatten out as you get older, and unless you're going to have it surgically lifted, there's not much you can do about it. With my customers, after a certain age, we're always lifting the skirts up at the waistband in the back because when there is no backside to fill it out, the skirts really do droop. Now that's when youth has really fled!

Wide hips, on the other hand, really can be a problem because—like the too-wide or too-narrow shoulder—they can throw off your proportions. The advent of slimmer pants has helped women a lot. Those baggy, man-tailored trousers with all the pleats everywhere don't do anybody's hips any favors. There are very few women whose bodies don't pull on those pleats, and then you add pockets on the sides, which just makes everything pull even more. If you're going to wear pants, wear slim ones. This floppy stuff looks terrible. The best-fitting, most flattering pants (especially good for slimming down wide hips) is the old-fashioned side-zipper pant. You get a much cleaner, flatter, leaner look across the middle because the front is totally smooth. And here's the best trick of all: Take out all of the pockets. Any tailor can snip them out and sew up the seam flat. If you just take those pockets out, I swear you can lose a quarter-inch off your hips.

If your problem lies more in the tummy than the hips, the best foil is any sort of top that hits right at the hipbone. It could be a square-shaped sweater that hangs freely straight to the hip (avoid the ones that bind at the bottom), a single-breasted jacket, or a sleeveless vest. You also have to get over the notion that anything that isn't nipped in at the waist automatically looks like maternity wear. It really is a wonderfully comfortable way to dress, and nothing hides a stomach as well as a great-looking shirt that's cut on the diagonal to fall away from the body, worn over a pair of slim-fitting trousers.

Pregnant women are truly tough customers, because so many of them are loath to resort to maternity clothes—and who can blame them, since most are so unfashionable and unbecoming? I say wear real clothes for as long as you possibly can, but eventually you will be forced to look to the maternity stores, at least for bottoms. Pick up a couple of pairs of slim-legged maternity pants, leggings, or narrow skirts that can serve as the foundation for your entire pregnancy wardrobe. You can then top them off with a variety of nonmaternity options— from crisp men's shirts (on their own or under a big cardigan or vest) to an A-line sweater or a mandarin collar jacket that's pulled in at the neck but flows out from there. If you can't find any tuniclike shirts or jackets that are wide enough to accommodate your belly, they are easy to create. Just take a full silk shirt and have your tailor make four- to five-inch slits up both side seams. Dresses can also be a great solution—and they don't always have to be from the maternity store. Look for A-line dresses in flowing fabrics and anything with an Empire waist to give the illusion of shape without feeling tight or constricting.

The real trick to feeling good about yourself during your pregnancy is to dress to

Maternity is beautiful! —dress it up!

show off whatever still looks good. If you've kept your shapely legs, then shorten your skirts a bit (remember to have the hem taken up more in the back than the front or it'll be lopsided). If you like the look of your increased bosom, then try on a scoop-necked top. And don't be afraid to bare your arms. Even if you normally hate them, this is one time when they are guaranteed to look like sticks in comparison to the rest of you! Accessories too can help distract the eye—wear a bright scarf at the neck or an oversized pin or earrings to call attention to your face, not your belly.

These tricks will help iron out a few figure flaws, but don't be too disappointed if you get dressed, turn to the mirror, and still see only yourself—not Kate Moss—staring back at you. You can play a few clothes games, but you can't completely disguise what you are—nor should you. Dressing is not merely about finding camouflage, it's about finding what is becoming to your body. And then move on—there is more to life than what you wear!

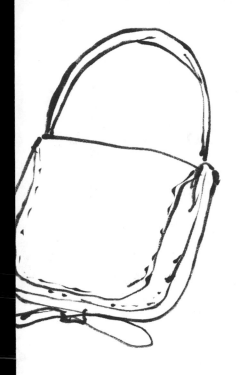

Chapter 3

WHY BASIC IS BORING

Part

1

THE
UNACCESSORIZED
LIFE IS NOT
WORTH LIVING

I was sitting in Betty's office putting together a wardrobe for a character that called for a very eclectic look. The clothing decisions were coming to a close, but the jewelry was still undecided. I kept saying the jewelry has to have style and size without being overwhelming— sort of like Betty's. With that, I looked at Betty and asked, "What about your jewelry? Let me buy it." Of course she looked at me like I was crazy, but off it came. Now that's personal shopping!
—Jeffrey Kurland,
  costume designer for
  Woody Allen films

To me, accessorizing is like painting. Your clothes become the frame and the necklace or the scarf or the earrings or whatever accessories you add become the artwork. I realize that this is a very difficult concept for a generation of minimalist dressers to come to grips with. If you're not used to wearing a lot of accessories (or any at all), you probably feel a little intimidated by the vast array of baubles you see when you walk through the jewelry department or peruse the old junk for sale at the flea market. But at the same time, you're probably also mesmerized by it. I had a customer the other day who was utterly entranced by all the remakes of antique Art Deco pins she was seeing in the store, but before she'd commit to buying one she wanted to go home and see what she could wear it with. I, on the other hand, would go the exact opposite route. I would buy the pin and then look for a way to dress myself around it. I say

get the pin, or the scarf or the shoes, first, and the outfit will

come later! It's a wonderful way to look at dressing.

I notice that people always comment on my jewelry—

especially the pins. I can't say that everyone actually *likes* them;

these aren't necessarily compliments, just comments. Wearing a

pin is a sure conversation starter. I have a pin, God knows how

long ago I got it, and if I paid a quarter for it, I'd be surprised.

It's just a little plastic thing—a red, white, and blue star. I can't

tell you how many times I've thought of ditching it, but I've

always just tossed it back in the drawer. When I went to a

luncheon recently, I stuck it on a red-and-white checked shirt,

and wouldn't you know, the next day one of the women called

me up to ask me where I'd gotten that pin! There's something

to be said for wonderful old junk.

I think that, innately, people love to adorn themselves. Just look around at different cultural and ethnic groups and age groups—each has its particular adornments, from pearl chokers to neck rings to pierced navels. Little children, who have no inhibitions and no fears yet of looking silly or overdone, are the best example because they can hardly stop bedecking themselves with their mother's jewelry, things that they make, junk they find, even the plastic "gems" that come out of Cracker Jack boxes. Unfortunately, when we grow up most of us lose sight of the fun aspect of fashion, and getting dressed—even when it comes to accessories—becomes a matter of mere practicality. That is no doubt why the best-selling accessories today are the functional ones: tote bags, watches, glasses. Things as seemingly superfluous as bracelets, pins, and scarves have fallen by the wayside. People get so wrapped up in thinking, "Do I need this?" But that's not what adornment is about. After all, when would you ever *need* a necklace? Never, of course, but that's exactly what makes it so much fun!

Buying jewelry should be like buying art. It's about collecting, and most people who like clothes do like to collect. If you are just beginning to discover accessories, remember that half the fun is in the search. It's about finding and falling in love with something that's pretty and makes you feel good when you put it on. Your eye will tell you immediately if it's beautiful—more so than with clothes, jewelry usually provokes an instant and distinct reaction. It's hard to feel ambivalent about something like an oversized lapel pin—you either love it or hate it on sight. And whether you're buying something real or fake, jewelry *should* be something you feel somewhat attached to, in a way you'll never feel about a sweater. There's no getting around the fact that jewelry is very sentimental and often has a lot of emotion attached to it. When your boyfriend or husband gives you jewelry for the first time, it's one of the most delicious experiences.

I'm not going to lay down a lot of hard-and-fast rules about how, when, and where to wear your accessories. The only rule I want you to establish is: Try it. Don't be shy about experimenting with a pin here or a scarf there. How far wrong can you really go?

BEDECKED AND BEJEWELED. Long ago, costume jewelry was considered the poor second cousin of the real thing, but Coco Chanel—who designed and wore a mix, both real and fake, of her signature strands of pearls—helped change all that. There's no doubt in my mind that costume jewelry is going to make a tremendous resurgence. Gucci dove into its archives and brought back the chain belt, and from there we go to faux gold and silver chain necklaces, huge stone rings, lapel pins with a spray of rhinestones and "emeralds," and so on. Costume jewelry, if not too expensive, can be thought of as disposable fashion. It's just for fun, you don't put it on like you're wearing something precious. It's a way to try on a new look without buying a new outfit: Add a chunky necklace to your old cocktail dress to give it new life; brighten up a black sweater with an armful of bold-colored Bakelite bracelets; or wear a funny pin to show the world you're in a whimsical mood.

And don't confine yourself to the traditional department store jewelry counters. Hunt through dime stores, your relatives' attics, thrift shops, antique shows, street vendors, flea markets, and even garage sales. With the renewed interest in the jewelry of the past, flea markets are often the best spot for picking up inexpensive trinkets. That's not to say that all costume jewelry is inexpensive (a new pair of Chanel faux pearl earrings can cost a few hundred dollars), and certainly all vintage costume jewelry is not (remember Jackie's faux pearl choker, which sold for thousands of dollars at Sotheby's). But if you have a keen eye, the patience to dig through *a lot* of junk, and a little imagination, there are plenty of treasures to be found.

Everyone obsesses about making sure all of their jewelry matches. God forbid they should have on gold earrings when they have a silver watch. I know that people hate to break up the set, but you shouldn't be too strict with yourself. The English aristocracy always mixed the sterling silver flatware with gold even in their most elaborate place settings. And then there is the jewelry (think of the Cartier rolling ring or the Rolex watch, for example) that mixes different tones of gold with silver, platinum, or stainless steel. It can look wonderful, so don't be too afraid to experiment. I'm never unsure of myself when I'm putting my jewelry on. It's not a matter of what goes together, because really it *all* goes together. I grab either a pin or a bead necklace first, that becomes the focal point, and then I build around it. I can accessorize myself in about three seconds flat, but I realize that you probably don't have the time to stand in front of the mirror holding up a dozen different pairs of earrings trying to make a decision. All I can do is urge you to take an extra minute to grab something and just try it—with security, and a little practice, you'll soon be able to accessorize yourself in no time.

Hoops

EARRINGS. Women of all ages can get addicted to earrings. They are one piece of jewelry that even accessory minimalists tend to gravitate toward. Someone said to me recently, "From now on, I'm going to buy earrings instead of clothes." Well, why not? Earrings can be flattering, fun, glamorous, and they can revitalize an old outfit—but they don't have to fit, and I've never known a pair of earrings that could make you look fat! Earrings are the easiest accessory to wear because they can be as unobtrusive or as dramatic as you like—from tiny diamond studs to elaborate oversized gold hoops to novelty styles that express a hobby or interest.

Since you have to start somewhere, I'd have to say that simple pearl earrings are the best first investment. They never go out of style, they make you feel dressed up even in jeans, but they will also go perfectly with any evening dress you ever wear. The only better basic for your jewelry wardrobe are diamond studs—a bit pricier than pearls, but hey, who says they have to be real? There are plenty of cubic zirconium copies out there that look beautiful, and I bet very few people will get close enough to your lobes to know the difference. Simple studs like these tend to look best on women with short, cropped hair (or a style that pulls hair away from the ears), because even two-karat diamonds can get a little lost in a mass of long hair. I'm partial to long, dangling, even outrageous earrings on anyone with long hair. They move and catch the light every time you throw a lock of hair over your shoulder or tuck it behind your ear.

NECKLACES. While a delicate chain always looks lovely against bare skin at the neck, we seem to be going back to the era of the *substantial* necklace—chunky gold chokers; single, double, and even triple strands of pearls; and big, big-beaded necklaces of many colors. These hefty chokers are not a challenge to wear because they can be wrapped around nearly any neckline (except a bulky turtleneck). And if you wear large matching earrings you will automatically feel you've completed your ensemble. That's not to say everything need match—especially with a pearl necklace (be it

What Works with What

- Round neckline: gold or silver cuff necklace; pearl or bead choker

- Low V neck: long, opera-length pearls; long, dangly necklace; or choker

- Boat neck: cuff necklace; opera-length pearls or beads; twisted-pearl strand choker

- Strapless: choker of big pearls or beads (wear two, one white and one black pearls) or elaborate "diamond and jewel" short necklace

- Turtleneck: cuff; long chain; pearl or bead necklace

real or fake), anything really goes. Pearls (even fake ones) do a wonderful thing for the complexion. Somehow they bring out the skin tones in a very flattering way. Not to mention what they do for clothes: Add a pearl choker to a simple open-necked dress, and suddenly it looks like it's worth a million dollars.

PINS. The one jewelry accessory I always encourage (and frequently wear myself) are lapel pins. Here is where you can really let your imagination run wild, and know that whatever you choose will become a conversation piece—which may explain why so many women are hesitant to try them. Pick something you identify with—an animal pin, an abstractly sculptural design, a flower, even a silk or real bloom (like the trademark Chanel camellias). For your first experiment, don't spend a fortune. Test the waters with a cheap flea market find—just pin it to your suit jacket and see if it doesn't soon become an almost daily part of dressing. If it makes it easier, you can even leave one pinned to your jacket when you hang it back up in the closet. That way you don't even have to think about accessorizing the next time you pull on that jacket.

Necklines

1. round neckline

2. long V-neck

3. boat neck

While the lapel is the most obvious spot to pin something, it is certainly not the *only* place you can wear a pin. If you have a top with a round neckline, try a pin right in the center of the neckline. You can even wear a shorter necklace above the pin, so that the pin becomes almost like a charm at the end of the necklace. Try a small pin on the collar of a blouse, an antique bar pin across the collar, or dress up a plain evening bag by sticking a glittery spray of "jewels" onto the front of it.

BRACELETS. There are some people who cannot stand feeling something around their wrists, and others who happily clang their way through life. I always think of the cat with the bell around his neck, because everyone hears me coming when I wear my favorite assortment of six or eight silver bangles around the office. There really is no way to sneak around if you wear a jangle of bangle, chain, or charm bracelets. Perhaps that's why more women take the conservative route and wear a single gold bangle, large cuff, or a simple tennis bracelet. If you do have a favorite that you wear every day, be sure to take it into

4. strapless

5. turtleneck

consideration when you buy a new jacket or long-sleeved dress. If the sleeves aren't shortened just enough to accommodate the bracelet, it will constantly catch on the fabric.

RINGS. I don't believe most people buy rings to go with their other jewelry, and rings are probably the one thing people don't worry about matching up with every other accessory. If you love your gold watch but have a platinum wedding ring, chances are, you will wear both—and chances are, it will look just fine! Rings are a wonderful way to accent your hands, and I have always felt that the hands are the most beautiful and expressive part of the body. You can layer rings as you would clothes, pick one extravagant, dazzling costume stone ring to dress up an evening dress, or use them to express sentimentality (your grandmother's signet ring or a school ring). So many women wear the same rings day in and day out without ever removing them—why not trade them on and off, experiment with something new, treat yourself to one as you would a scarf?

ABOUT TIME. It's practical. It conveys status. Plus, it's jewelry. A watch is the one accessory statement that most people make every day. I know women who wear one even when they're dressed for a black-tie party. It used to be that everyone had a work watch and then a daintier evening watch. Some people today are inclined to build an entire watch wardrobe consisting of a masculine tank-style watch, a sturdier one for sports and casual wear, and maybe a few novelty types just for fun. If you are going to invest in a piece of jewelry, a watch is a good place to put your money because not only is it something you'll wear nearly every day, but a classic watch is (if you'll pardon the pun) timeless. The famed "tank" (it doesn't have to be from Cartier, the originators of the tank) is a perfect example. You can easily find lookalikes in every price range—from the knockoff street vendors to Timex and Bulova on up. And a good-quality watch in a simple shape is all anyone really needs.

What the Swatch craze has taught us, however, is that watches don't have to be just about need, and they don't have to be classic in style. The trendy, inexpensive, colorful Swatch watches are being bought just for fun—it's a way to add a little liveliness to an outfit. Watches are also becoming collectibles. Once you get to a point where you've accumulated several different timepieces, a watch becomes a real fashion accessory—like a pair of earrings or a pin—that you change according to your outfit, your mood, or the season.

TIE ONE ON. Scarves are one of my favorite accessories. Wearing a scarf is a great way to update your old clothing and add something to a rather plain outfit—plus, a scarf automatically brings color and pattern into your wardrobe. A change of scarf can make a simple dress or suit look entirely different each time you wear it, which really helps to diversify and expand your wardrobe. When you shop for scarves, be sure to touch them—don't just look at the pattern and colors. It's the luxury of the fabric—soft cashmere, featherweight chiffon, buttery silk—that really makes the scarf. I think most of us admire scarves, and maybe even buy several, but there is a real knack to wearing them, and the average woman becomes all thumbs when it's time to put one on. There's nothing worse than being all dressed and not being able to fix the scarf. It's like the poor man all done up in his tuxedo and sweating over his bow tie.

How to Tie the Knot

Getting a scarf on correctly shouldn't require six hands. All it takes is a little know-how and a little practice. Here are several tying techniques you should be able to navigate and still make it to work on time.

- Use a barred ring (like the one Hermès designed for this purpose) to hold the scarf together; these are now available inexpensively at many scarf stores.

- Loop an elongated rectangle scarf just inside a jacket neckline.

- Fold a silk square in half (so it forms a triangle), wrap it around your head, and knot at the nape of the neck.

- Take a silk square, fold it into a triangle, then continue folding it over until you have a two-inch-wide sash to tie around your waist or hips.

- Any small scarf can be used as a pocket square to dress up a jacket.

- A really big scarf (like a stole or pareo) can be extremely versatile. Wrap a sheer chiffon or silk pareo around your chest and tie it above the bosom for a chic beach cover-up. Fling a cashmere or dressy organza stole over a cocktail dress in lieu of a coat.

ring w· bar

rectangle scarf
inside jacket

stole or pareo

The most practical scarf, and the easiest to wear, is the large shawl—like the sort Halston popularized in the seventies. A truly wonderful invention, it comes in such a variety of fabrics (from casual wool tartans to lightweight taffetas to luxurious cashmeres or even fur) that you can wear one on any number of occasions. Throw a fancy one over an evening dress if you don't own a dressy enough coat, or pack a warm wool shawl when you travel in the fall. It's much more space-efficient than stuffing a coat in your bag, and it will keep you just as warm on cool nights. Large shawls in nice fabrics (especially luxury fabrics like cashmere) can be very costly, but they really are a great investment because the style never changes (it's just a big rectangle) and you really can wear them over anything.

Scarf dressing shouldn't be intimidating—if you have them, wear them! What mistakes can you possibly make? The big, printed silk square (like the classic Hermès) is the style most often bought, and it really is incredibly versatile and easy to wear. For starters, just fold it in half into a triangle and wrap it around your neck. It's an ideal way to show off the print or scene on the scarf, and better yet, it's absolutely foolproof. But the beauty of this size scarf is that you can also fold it into a narrow strip and use it as a sash belt, tie it around your chest as a bandeau, wrap it around your head Jackie O–style. The possibilities are truly endless. You can even fake the scarf look with a three-quarter-yard rectangle of fabric—a lovely silk, soft chiffon, or antique lace. Take the piece and

tuck it around the inside neckline of a suit jacket instead of wearing a blouse.

FOUR EYES. Maybe back in Dorothy Parker's day men didn't make passes at girls who wore glasses, but today, eyewear—whether it's corrective glasses or celebrity-style sunglasses—is one hot accessory. With all of the famous names now endorsing frames, glasses have become yet another status accessory. From high-end and high-priced frames like Giorgio Armani to the name brands like Sophia Loren and Pierre Cardin that are available at every optical chain store, glasses are an easy way to buy yourself a little bit of designer chic. I like to think of buying glasses the way I would of buying a frame for a picture—you want the frame to complement, but not distract from, what's inside.

however... men do make passes at girls who wear sunglasses!

scarf →

   Thin, wire-framed glasses are perfect for women with small faces, or anyone who wants their glasses to fade into the background. On the other hand, there are plenty of women who wear big, bold frames as a fashion signature. It depends really on what you are comfortable with, and there's no rule that says you can't have it both ways—collect a few pairs of frames and change them as the mood strikes you. I don't think haircuts should dictate what frames you wear—it's all a matter of what you like when you turn to the mirror. And if you are forced to wear reading glasses (the great indignity of the over-forty set!), don't shy away from the old "grandmother chain." Adorned with tortoiseshell links, beads, leather, and bright stones, these chains have become quite a chic solution to keeping your glasses handy.

BAG LADIES. You can approach handbags in two ways: One is to put your wallet on the block, extend yourself, and really invest in an expensive bag in a classic shape and basic color—and then vow never to change your handbag. The other approach is to

Bags

make several, smaller-ticket purchases to put together a
wardrobe of bags in a variety of colors, shapes, sizes, and
patterns to go with different outfits and pick up on current
trends. There's no right or wrong approach; it depends more on
your personal style. Are you generally conservative in your
dressing, preferring to have one do-everything bag to carry
every day? Then invest. If you're more inclined to change bags
as often as you change clothes, then be careful not to get lured
by bags that are both too pricey and too trendy. You'll end up
with closets full of "last year's bag" that you no longer feel chic
carrying.

Investing in a good bag makes sense for a variety of
reasons. One that's large enough to carry to work every day
takes a lot of wear and tear, so it needs to be high quality. It's
also very visible. Like an overcoat (except that a bag is used all
year round), your bag is part of the first impression people get
of your style, taste, and even personality. (Let's face it, we do
read a lot into people's clothing, don't we?) I think that's why so
many women will even shell out money for a statusy "label"
bag—like Coach, Louis Vuitton, Prada, Gucci, or Chanel—it's
a security blanket. By carrying a recognizable name brand,
you're announcing your good taste (and maybe wealth) to
everyone you pass by on the street. Now of course I'm not
trying to suggest that the only reason women buy expensive
bags is that they're insecure. Spending a lot on a bag buys you
much more than just status. You get a product that is made
from the most luxurious materials, has a stunning design, and
features first-class quality and workmanship. *That* is why it's
called investment dressing. When buying an expensive everyday
bag, look to the conservative colors—black, navy, brown,
burgundy, tan. But don't think you have to have a black bag just
because you're wearing black clothing. I love a camel or beige

leather bag as an accessory to dark clothes, and I'm also a big believer in wearing navy accessories (like shoes and a bag) with black clothes. It's an old European concept, and it looks very chic.

The backpack—now officially co-opted by the fashionable set—has definitely moved from the worlds of sport and the school yard into its current role as a totally acceptable everyday alternative to the tote bag or large purse. I see well-dressed women of every age group lugging these bags, stuffed with entire lives—their precious Filofaxes, cell phones, maybe even a change of clothing. And while I understand the practicality of carrying such a big bag, I think it may be time to stage a return to the more feminine handbag. Those oversized ones can be lethal to the person walking next to you on the street if you happen to turn your shoulders—*whack!* Here's my advice: If you have a lot to carry, stow all your belongings plus a little handbag in the backpack. Then when you go out during the day or after work, you only need to bring your necessities in the little bag to lunch or dinner.

When you're looking for fashion that's just for the moment, don't discount the street vendors selling their (sometimes very good) knockoffs of chic Prada, Gucci, etc. More women are cutting back on the number of bags they own, so these inexpensive fakes are a good way to add an occasional boost without investing in the real thing. The street vendors are very up on the current trends. What's wrong with buying something cheap that looks good and makes you feel statusy for a bit? It's fun, and who cares if it doesn't last forever? An evening bag is another place you can easily get away with spending less money. Granted there are a lot of truly spectacular, outrageously expensive evening bags out there— Judith Leiber's bejeweled miniatures, Prada's silk pouches,

Chanel's quilted clutches. But you can also find simple, inexpensive faille or poly-satin bags at the last minute at any department or even discount clothing store. Another great resource for dressy bags are vintage stores. I can't tell you how many friends ask to borrow my old evening bags—I keep them all and have a collection that includes petit point beaded bags that were my mother's from back in the 1930s and '40s.

WAIST NOT. Many of us automatically grab a belt and wrap it around any piece of clothing that comes with belt loops. While it does seem a shame to let those loops sit empty, using a belt to your figure's and your outfit's advantage requires more than just finding a strip of leather that will fit through the loops. With the resurgence of belts as a real fashion accessory in recent seasons, the waist has become yet another spot to add a bit of status to an outfit. The Hermès "H" buckle belt is a long-standing classic. The Gucci belt with the signature horse-bit buckle (and the myriad knockoffs available at every price level) sells out on a regular basis. And a few seasons ago when the skinny patent belt was all the rage for every fashionable waist, stores around the country had waiting lists for the coveted Calvin Klein version.

Many women are afraid to cinch themselves in the middle because they don't want to call attention to their hips or to a thick waist. The waist is, after all, the first thing to go as we age—not many women retain their Scarlett O'Hara proportions for life. Which is exactly why most of my customers have the belt loops taken off of all the pants and skirts they buy (this a simple thing any tailor can do). I mean, after all, when is a belt really used for its original function anyway? I don't know a single person who's ever lost their pants walking down the street because they didn't have a belt on! I think as you lose your waist, wearing a belt becomes very uncomfortable. No one wants to be that uncomfortable anymore just for the sake of fashion. Years ago we had those big girdle belts with the four-inch-wide buckle that dug into you every time you sat down. Your rib cage would be black and blue by the end of an evening. But we're not living in that era anymore—Scarlett is dead and gone.

Belts are not a necessary investment, but if you love them and feel comfortable in them, you should splurge on a good skin belt—reptile or alligator (the embossed leather kind can be just as beautiful at a fraction of the price). You'll wear it on all of your trousers, even jeans and khakis, plus wrap it around the waist of a shirtwaist dress or slim knit dress. Another good basic is a chain belt—which you can find in gold, silver, and even with links of tortoiseshell. The beauty of the chain or long leather cord belt is that it's not designed to cinch you tightly at the waist. These are meant to be worn slightly looser so that they sit closer to the hips. You'll be amazed at how this can distract from a large waist and make it seem smaller in proportion.

Once you've accumulated a few basics, you can start to build up a collection of novelty belts. Use them as adornment—that's the fun part. Find ones that are almost like a piece of jewelry or art. I have a drawer full of old belt buckles I've cut off and saved because they were so unusual. (Somehow the belts got smaller, but the buckles remained the same!) I have old Jean Muir ones that are so beautiful—she was known for them. Someday I'll have a new leather strip put on the old buckles. I've had a belt made out of feathers for years—it is the most gorgeous belt you've ever seen. I used to wear it on knit dresses. That's when belts are exciting—when you find ones that liven up an outfit and that you want to collect and hold on to forever.

Part 2

THE SHOE FETISH

As a working woman with very little free time, Solutions with Betty Halbreich is my ultimate solution. I can always get the perfect outfit for any event without the trauma of shopping tirelessly.
—Sylvia Weinstock, Sylvia Weinstock Cakes, Ltd.

Women probably love shoes as an accessory more than anything else. Sure they have to fit your foot, but they don't have to fit like a dress. They don't require analysis with the help of a three-way mirror. When you put on a pair of shoes, you don't have to worry about how your behind looks or if they make your stomach look fat or whether or not you're having a bad-hair day. I know women who are a size twenty but collect the most amazing pairs of shoes. Shoes are the perfect thing to buy, a way to feel you have something new when you don't want to buy clothes. And yes, of course, shoes absolutely have to be practical and comfortable on some level. My mother always says that if your shoes hurt you wear them on your face. And while that may be true, you don't have to forsake style and excitement for comfort. The real fun of buying shoes comes most often from finding a pair that doesn't seem very practical at all. I love to buy a divine pair of shoes—even if I have nothing to wear them with—and then dress myself from the feet up. After all, what's more wonderful than buying an exciting pair of shoes, something you wouldn't ordinarily buy but maybe found on the sale rack, and then building an outfit to showcase them?

During the slow clothes-buying seasons, I'll walk through the store and every department will be nearly empty. All except for the shoe department, which is as bustling as a toy store at Christmas. I think that no matter how many clothes a woman has, there is always room in her wardrobe for another pair of shoes. As I walk around the streets of New York and see all of the women rushing off to work in their running sneakers, I often wonder where

all these beautiful shoes go. But that said, nothing livens up an old outfit like a stylish new pair of shoes. I also think that women are willing to open their wallets up a bit wider when it comes to shoes. Let's face it: Any pair of shoes is expensive these days. But I'm constantly amazed to see women crowded around the Prada and the Gucci (at $200, $300, and even $400 a pair) displays. Even at those prices, it is still cheaper to buy shoes than a whole designer outfit, so for the woman who can't or won't spend $2,000 on the Calvin Klein suit, the $300 designer pumps are her way of investing in some top-of-the-line chic. I truly believe that beautiful shoes *do* make a difference in how you look no matter how much you spend on the rest of your clothes, and if you care for them properly, they can also have tremendous longevity. There can be a lot more originality and versatility with shoes as well. Gone are the days of the black pump with the black suit, the navy pump with the navy suit, and so on. Especially with people traveling so much these days and not wanting to pack a half dozen pairs of shoes, those old rules seem ridiculous.

Although many women have closets piled full of shoes, here is what I would consider a good, basic beginner's wardrobe of shoes.

•**A simple black shoe** (probably a mid-heeled leather pump of some sort) to wear with basically everything.

•**Sneakers** for whatever sport or activity you do, even if that means just walking around town.

•A pair of **casual shoes** in black, brown, or navy (depending on the predominant colors in your wardrobe), like a loafer or chunky lace-up shoe, to wear with weekend clothes like jeans and khakis as well as with pantsuits to work on more casual days.

•A pair of very dressy **evening shoes** to wear to cocktail parties, weddings, and other fancy occasions. These can be dreadfully expensive, but think of them as part of your investment dressing and plan to hold on to evening shoes for years to come.
•And finally, your basic shoe wardrobe should allow for at least one pair (two if you can afford it or find them on sale) of the newest, most **stylish shoes of the season.** It's such an easy way to pick up on a trend and feel suddenly "in."

Not only can a fabulous new pair of shoes give a lift to an old outfit, they can also change your appearance and perspective on yourself. Take the woman who always wears flat shoes or pumps with a small, "sensible" heel. If you make her slip into a higher-heeled pump with a light, sheer stocking on her legs, I guarantee she'll feel suddenly sexier and probably run right out and have all of her skirts shortened. What I'm trying to say is that the right shoes can really change your look. And just as heels can elongate your legs, the right pair of man-tailored oxfords can add a new sense of authority (not to mention comfort) to your pantsuits.

The first thing every customer says to me after I find her a dress or help her put together a new wardrobe is: Betty, what shoes do I wear? And then immediately after that it's: What stockings do I wear? Stocking decisions provoke the same fear as accessorizing yourself with a pin or a bracelet—and most women need help. Shoes and stockings can be a tremendous accessory, but you have to learn to go beyond the basics of black, brown, and taupe. That said, opaque black tights are one of the best things to happen to fashion (and women's legs) in recent history. They really do hide a multitude of sins. They can make heavy legs look slimmer, plus they cover up all the veins and spots our legs take on over the years.

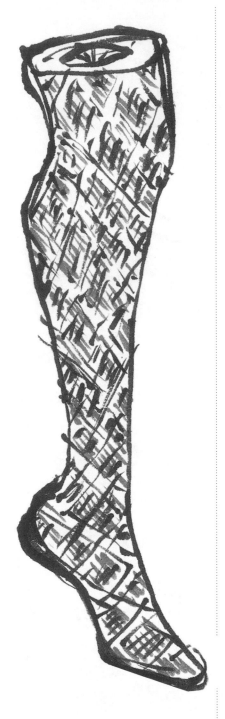

You really aren't taking full advantage of all the varieties of panty hose out there if you just stick to the basics. I love them all and consider them a wonderful accessory. An accessory which—maybe because it's also such a day-to-day necessity—is often underrated from a fashion point of view. But next time you're out shopping, take a few minutes to really look around the stocking department rather than just rushing in and replenishing your supply of boring beiges and blacks. Examine the samples, check out the different textures, weights, and colors. It's an especially good idea to do this at the start of the new season. Just five minutes of perusing the stocking department will give you a quick education on what colors and patterns are big. And as long as you are right there looking at them all, why not take home a few pairs (something other than what you normally buy) and experiment with them? This is one instance where a very important piece of clothing—one that has the power to instantly update a look—is truly affordable to all.

Spring and summer are the times when we all grow to hate the idea of tugging panty hose on every day. If you have the legs to do it (and it's acceptable in your office), then take advantage of the warm weather to go without. But if you really feel that you want or need a little light covering on your legs all year round, opt for some of the new, almost invisible sheers. I like to think of them in the same way I do foundation for the face: Neither should make you look like you're wearing anything, yet somehow they manage to make your skin (and your legs) look nearly flawless. Many of these sheer stockings have a bit of shimmer to them, which is a beautiful—and almost fragile—look for evening, but the matte versions are great for the office with a suit or dress.

As soon as fall and winter roll around, that's when panty hose and thicker tights start to get really interesting. Out come all of the rich, autumn tones, the intricate patterns, and luxurious textures designed to complement the heavier, woollier clothes of the season. The dark opaques—in burgundy, navy, brown, forest green, and of course, black—are good staples for a cool-weather wardrobe. Not only do they blend well with the colors of the clothes, but the thicker weights will actually help keep you warm when you decide to wear a short skirt on a blustery winter day. I'll often correspond the color of the pantyhose with the color of a top. For example: a dark green sweater set, black skirt, dark green tights. It helps to pull the whole look together as an outfit.

I know women have been brainwashed that, unless you're wearing sheer stockings, then the shoes and the panty hose must be a perfect match. I say to hell with those so-called rules! Of course there are times when it looks great to put, say, a brown opaque stocking with brown shoes. It gives you a very elongated, leggy look that's especially great with a short skirt. But let's say you're wearing a gray flannel suit with a chocolate brown top under the jacket and brown suede pumps. Dark brown stockings would look too heavy and would drag the whole outfit into drabness. Instead, try a blackish taupe stocking that adds a little color to the leg but doesn't compete with the rest of the look.

If you want to get really adventurous with panty hose, then you should definitely look into different textures and patterns in addition to different colors. You can play with patterns by wearing ribbed tights with a plaid skirt or maybe herringbone tights with a nubby, tweed suit. Chunky-looking

cable knits can be found in thinner stocking versions (more flattering to the leg) and they look wonderful with a woolly sweater dress or a camel hair jumper. Even fishnet stockings have made a comeback. My advice: If you want to try fishnets, wear another pair of tights underneath them (sheer, opaque, colored, whatever) because otherwise the fishnets will be cutting into your feet all day long. Ouch!

MAKING THE MOST OF MOTHER NATURE

When you come right down to it, your best accessories may be those you were born with. And by that I mean your own face and your hair. Of course, both usually look better when you give your natural assets a little boost—such as investing in a great haircut, treating yourself to a professional facial, or applying some subtle makeup. I know that this sort of attention to cosmetic details makes women feel better, because every time I have a customer who is really pleased with what she's just bought, she will immediately run down to the makeup counter to try on a different color lipstick or buy a new shade of nail polish. In fact, I rarely see an empty makeup counter—women seem to flock to those testers and free makeovers. After all, makeup is a wonderful accessory (and just like fashion, the "in" colors seem to change every season), so investing in a new lipstick is probably the simplest and least expensive way of picking up on a new trend and making yourself feel stylish.

Years ago I used to have someone come up from the cosmetics floor to do makeup on my customers after they'd bought something new. Now I try to stay out of it even though women do still ask my advice about what color lipstick they should wear with a particular dress. With all the choices now it's become much more personalized. I find most of the women I know are so busy wearing that sort of no-makeup makeup that takes hours to put on, and they certainly don't want to be told they need more color on their face. But I really do think that color will return. I think that low-key, I'm-not-wearing-any-makeup look has just about *that* much life left in it. If you look around at the young people you'll see all of the incredibly bold-colored nail polish they're wearing—blue, gold, purple. If it started with the toes and moved up to the fingers, where's the next place it's going to hit?

I'm a dime store person myself. I grew up using Max Factor makeup, and I don't see anything wrong with it. All makeup manufacturers market similar colors. Especially now, the trickle down from the high-priced lines happens overnight—just like it does with fashion. I think it's terrific. What that means is that now everyone is allowed to be as fashionable as she wants, and it doesn't matter where you shop. I don't care if it's Target or Bergdorf Goodman.

As long as you're taking the care to flatter your face with a little makeup, you should also not forget about the rest of your body. Services like facials, massages, manicures, and pedicures are the ultimate treats you can give yourself. God knows we work hard enough, don't we all deserve to luxuriate once in a while? Even if you can't or don't

BRUSH

polish

want to spend the money on the professional salon services (although I strongly recommend a deep-cleansing facial every few months; it really wakes up your skin tones), take a few minutes each week to treat yourself to at-home versions. It's easy enough to give yourself a manicure and pedicure using the tools (a file, cuticle stick, pumice stone, base and top coats, and polish) available at any drugstore. I guarantee you can do it in the time it takes to sit and watch your favorite sitcom.

But while makeup and manicures may be nice extras, a good haircut is truly a necessity. I had a new customer—a beautiful woman with a great wardrobe and excellent taste— but she really needed a haircut. I didn't have the nerve to say anything to her because it was the first time I was working with her, but usually I will say something because I think it's *that* important to your overall look. I can put someone in the greatest outfit you've ever seen, but if her hair is a mess or outdated or overly damaged, it really will detract from her look. It's a huge plus to reevaluate your hairstyle at least once a year. Especially if you are going through a transitional stage in your life (starting a job, getting promoted, getting married) and are planning to invest in a new wardrobe. Better to have your hair done before you decide to go shopping. When you do, it's like walking into the store and announcing, I have just had my haircut, I'm new from the neck up, and now I need something for the rest of me.

If you want to be adventurous and

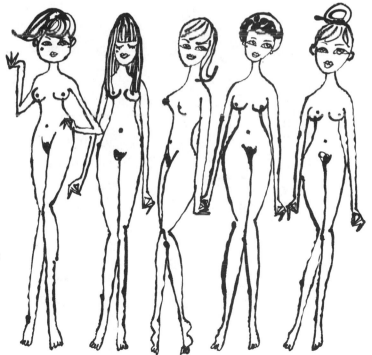

I've just had my haircut: Now Dress Me!

really change your image, the most obvious place to start is with your hair. You really can change your whole look by cutting it. You're one person when you walk into the salon and you can become a totally different person by the time you emerge. A new haircut can allow you to dress differently, say different things, try out new makeup. It gives you a whole new sense of freedom. I've seen women suddenly willing to change their clothing style and try new things after changing their hair. Maybe they decide to wear pants if they never did before. Or they decide to experiment with something sexier or try on a bolder color than they'd ever dared to wear before. I often say that a new haircut is like a new piece of jewelry—both can change your look and both can help revitalize your same old outfits.

Now granted, it is, as an old friend of mine liked to remind me, only hair. And if you get a bad cut, it'll come back in a few months. But that said, a good haircut is often worth spending a bit more money on. You've got to find someone good to cut it, and that's not always going to be your neighborhood place. And you definitely want to steer clear of these factorylike places where each client is given a fifteen-minute time slot and the stylists simply churn out an assembly line of cookie-cutter haircuts with little regard for your particular wants, your face shape, or your hair's texture. So the cut is where you really should open up your purse a little wider. Now you don't necessarily have to keep going back to the expensive, high on the totem pole, man of the moment haircutter every six to eight weeks for your trims. What I'd suggest doing is, as soon as you get a haircut you really love, go to your local hairdresser and show him your head. Let him see the cut as it is meant to look rather than waiting till it's all grown out and then making him try to re-create something he's never seen. That way, when it is time for a trim, you can go to your local hairdresser and trust him to clean up your cut.

Following the lead of movie actresses (who change for every part) and supermodels like Linda Evangelista, more and more women are using hair color as an accessory—the way people used to use lipstick or nail polish. In fact some actually change it *that* often. I'm not a huge believer in this, mostly because I don't think it's very healthy for the hair, but there is nothing wrong with changing your color periodically to suit your mood or the current fashion. Just be careful not to get so wrapped up in the color of your hair that you neglect color in your wardrobe. I have one customer who will wear only the blandest palette of navy and black because she is so worried about her clothes clashing with her hair. She's a chameleon from the neck up (I've seen her go from blond to chestnut to red to brown), but from the neck down she's totally set in her ways.

Granted there is a lot of insecurity when it comes to hair, but I still don't believe people should be overly attached to one hairdresser or one hairstyle. I think that half the fun is experimenting. Just try something new! There are very few people who are so well coiffed that you stop to take a second look at them. When I see a great haircut or someone with a really gorgeous haircolor, I turn around to get another look. And often I go up to someone to compliment her or find out who cut it, because truly great hair is something that strikes me—even more so than whatever she's wearing. Isn't hair supposed to be our crowning glory? Well, then treat it that way!

Chapter

BLACK

BEAUTIF

Part

1

Top Ten Reasons Why Black Is Always Better

1. It never goes out of style. (In other words, if you're going to splurge on a big investment item, make it black.)

2. It goes with everything.

3. You can wear the same black dress, suit, skirt, pants, or sweater five times a week and hardly anyone will notice.

4. You can wear it for years and only need to dry-clean it twice.

5. Even a red wine spill can't ruin it.

6. It really does make you look thinner.

7. It looks expensive—even if it's not.

8. You can wear it all year round, in any weather, to any event.

REVEALING YOUR DARK SIDE

Everyone in the fashion business—from the designers to the magazine editors to the department store buyers—loves to complain about how fashion has gotten so boring in recent years because everyone always wears black. And then every couple of seasons the magazines nearly trip over themselves in their excitement to announce that *color is back!* Well, if you've ever been to a fashion runway show (just take a look at the audience the next time you see clips of one on VH-I or MTV's *House of Style*), you know the fashion industry's not-so-well-kept secret, because the entire, and I mean *entire*, audience is wearing head-to-toe black. All those so-called trendsetters and fashion dictators can't seem to break away from basic black—even as parades of models in lovely shades strut past them, even as they write about how modern whatever the shade of the season is, even as they talk to the designers about how wonderful women look in colors. And there is a good reason for this fashionable love affair with black; in fact, there are dozens of good reasons for it. And I'd be lying through my teeth if I didn't come right out and say that black is beautiful. It's timeless. It's practical. It's sexy. It's slimming. And most of all, it's *simple*.

I love lighter colors and seasonal colors that change with the weather. Having learned my color sense from my mother, I've never been afraid to wear a mix of beautiful shades, and I still gravitate toward my favorite colors when I walk into the sweater department. But I'm a working woman. And like other working women, I get out of bed in the morning, and need to get dressed in a hurry; the easiest thing for me to reach for is black. Of course, unlike most minimalist, black-addicted women, I rarely wear an unadorned, somber, black-on-black

9. You get to wear those miraculous, hide-everything opaque black stockings with it.

10. You always match.

voila!

you always match!

Ten Ways to Liven Up Your Basic Black

1. Loop an animal-print scarf around your neck or wrap an animal-print belt around your waist.

2. Add a chunky gold or silver chain at your neck.

3. Try on a different color and/or texture of stockings.

4. Take this opportunity to wear those bright pink shoes that you think don't go with anything.

5. Ditto that red patent handbag you bought on sale.

6. Wear a sweater or shirt in your favorite color under a black suit.

7. A choker of pearls or colored beads can add interest to a low neckline.

8. Mix in a little texture as well as color to dress a black suit up or down (like a silk shantung shirt for evening or a nubby wool sweater for the weekend).

9. Don't be afraid to mix black pieces with other neutral basics like navy shoes or a brown belt.

combination. To me, black is easy because it works as a bland backdrop to everything else I pile on top of it—be it my large silver insect lapel pin, a neckful of beads, my usual jangle of bracelets, or a brilliant-colored sweater.

But I know that the reason everyone else automatically grabs black every morning is that it doesn't really require much thought. It simplifies your entire closet, simplifies your shopping trips, and eliminates the need for frequent stops at the dry cleaners (black hides many secrets, including dirt). You really don't need to own as many clothes when you predominantly stick to wearing black because no one really knows for sure if you are wearing the same ones over and over. And as an added, money-saving asset, a black wardrobe allows you to get away with a single handbag (black, of course) and one or two pairs of shoes (in you-know-what).

Actually, the only truly difficult thing about wearing a lot of black is figuring out how to grab the right piece of clothing in the morning from a closet that looks like a sea of similar dark pieces. But I don't care what its detractors say, all black clothing does *not* look alike. You learn to distinguish one black dress from another by the style and the fit. Or maybe you just brainwash yourself into thinking, "I'm not really putting on another black outfit today, I'm putting on my knit suit" or "I'm wearing that sexy tight dress." That's how you distinguish one piece of black clothing from another.

I have a friend who's cloaked in black every single day, and I mean cloaked, from her hair to her glasses to her clothes to her shoes. People say she always looks like she's dressed for Halston's funeral. Now there's no doubt about it, she looks chic—in a very sort of New York City–chic way. But no matter how much you like to hide behind that security blanket of all black, you've *got* to break up the monotony every once in a while. If you wear black, think of it as just the frame—the picture inside the frame needs some interesting touches. Black, being as conservative as it is—and, let's face it, sometimes even boring—needs embellishment. To start, you need to have a good haircut. A good pair of earrings, good shoes, and a good handbag (and you can use those accessories as a way of adding at least a touch of subtle or bold color).

If I wander into my more analytical role as fashion therapist, I'd have to say that underneath all the perfectly good, sound, logical, and sensible reasons for wearing black is the one darker (excuse the pun) reason that no one wants to admit. Insecurity. Women—even the most seemingly self-confident and fashionable—feel safe in black. They feel appropriate. They know they'll look good, but won't stand out from the crowd. Let's face it, it's a lot scarier and takes a lot more courage to walk into a party wearing a skintight red dress than it does wearing a skintight black one. And the same goes for a business suit. Who wants to be the only one at the board meeting not to blend into the sea of dark hues? I have customers who come in and say to me, Betty, I absolutely can't buy any more black. But the customer is usually just mouthing the words. She's become extremely secure in black and is too scared to venture anywhere else. For that woman, to go to any of the brighter, sharper colors can have a jarring effect. It's culture shock.

So the question is: How do you break up that wall of black without feeling *too* colorful and too vulnerable? The solution is to not go from one extreme to the other in the course of one outfit. If people are used to seeing you in head-to-toe black, of course you'll stand out like crazy if you all of a sudden show up one day in head-to-toe fuschia. As with most addictions, going cold turkey is the toughest route. Ease your

10. Test a color you think you wouldn't normally wear by putting it with an all-black suit. Like seafoam green, which, if it doesn't have too much yellow in it, is a refreshing change from the usual white or red you normally pair with black.

How to Know When You Have Enough

- You know what they say about too much of a good thing, and yes, that old wisdom applies even to your closet.

- People you barely know come up to console you for your recent loss.

- Your friends tell you you look vibrant when you show up in charcoal gray instead of black.

- Even you stop being able to tell your clothes apart.

- You have to install a fluorescent light in your closet because the overwhelming darkness of the clothes makes it impossible to see a thing.

- Going shopping gets boring because the black things you automatically reach for really do all start to look the same.

way out of black and into color *gradually*. Add a little color here and there to liven things up. But don't feel like you ever have to leave your beloved black behind completely. God knows, some of the world's most fashionable and best-dressed women never have . . . and most likely never will.

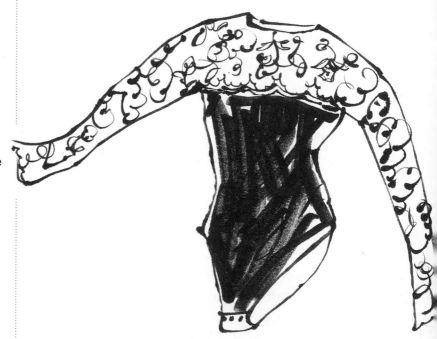

BREAKING UP
IS HARD TO DO

I'm always amazed at how many women are terrified to mix up their wardrobes. I look in their closets (and maybe yours looks this way too) and there they are—all the prematched "outfits" hung up together in a long line like little soldiers. It's like those Garanimals clothes they used to make for kids that came with animal-coded tags: Anything with a lion tag went with anything else with a lion tag. But if one tag had a monkey and another had a lion, then that was wrong and you couldn't put them together. Now that may be fine for five-year-olds, but why are we, as grown ups, so afraid to let all the different species intermingle? Okay, sometimes it does spawn a monster of an outfit, but, done correctly, mixing up your pieces is the best, easiest, and cheapest way to extend your wardrobe. Not to mention the best way to break an all-black addiction without putting yourself, or those used to seeing you in the dark, into shock.

The Do's and Don'ts of Mix and Match

• Wear a boxy suit jacket over jeans and you'll look like a box with denim legs.

• Not all colors (even of the same shade) are created equal: Before you try to wear that maroon jacket with the pair of maroon trousers you found in the back of the closet, be sure they really do match.

• Fitted jackets and straight skirts are a nearly foolproof combination.

• Just because Ungaro and Geoffrey Beene are known for mixing bold pattern on top of bold pattern doesn't mean you should try this on your own. Chances are, people will think you're

→

colorblind before they think you're wearing a Beene original.

- Don't be fooled by artistic magazine photo shoots: Wildly clashing colors all worn together in the same outfit (like a red jacket with a pink sweater and orange pants) rarely look chic.

- Classic, man-tailored trousers can be safely mixed with most jackets, sweater sets, and even simple T-shirts.

- A full skirt worn with a slouchy, unstructured jacket will make you look eight months pregnant no matter how thin you are.

- Dressy and casual is a tough mix. A soft wool cardigan can look great with a taffeta evening skirt, but don't try to top off a wool gabardine skirt with a taffeta jacket and wear it to work.

With black you really do get a lot of value for your money on several different levels. For one thing, black hides a multitude of sins—not just in your figure—but in the construction of the garment itself. With colored clothing, if the garment is not extremely well made and cut from beautiful fabric, its flaws are more blatant. The stitching is more obvious, the placement of the pockets, the seams—it all shows through. But in black, it all seems to fade in. To prove it to yourself, go to the store and hold up five black skirts (in all different prices, from bargain basement to designer). I challenge you to tell the difference between them. Try this same experiment with, for example, a pastel pink skirt and chances are you would know the cheap one from the expensive one in an instant.

The other value-adding feature of black is the way you are able to take your various black pieces and mix them up. And I think with the high prices of clothes today it's becoming more and more important to own clothes that you are able to use in many ways. In other words, to make them worth the money, your clothes have to have more than one life. Take the example of a woman who came to me the other day for a dress to wear out to dinner. She ended up buying a little black sleeveless shift dress that came with a fitted jacket to wear over it. Well, she can wear that outfit as it is to dinner or a party, or she can wear the dress alone and fancy it up with a scarf or necklace for dressier occasions.

But the real beauty of it is that that's not the only way to use the outfit. I told her to go home and look at her other skirts. By slipping the jacket over a white shirt and pairing it with more casual straight or pleated skirts, she's got new "suits" to wear to work. If she takes the dress and tosses other jackets or a cardigan over it, she's got even more outfits. That's the way you get real value out of your clothes. If you can buy one outfit and suddenly be able to create a half a dozen more—by mixing the new pieces with those already hanging in the closet—you know you've made a wise investment. And in the process, you've also found the secret for breaking up the monotony of black without having to forsake it altogether.

We all need neutrals in our wardrobe. Even a woman who absolutely adores color and wears a rainbow of shades on any given day needs some sort of foundation around which to build those colorful outfits. You would look pretty silly if you were always wearing a kaleidoscope of hues. Picture it: a pink jacket, yellow top, with a navy skirt, and tan shoes. But that same pink jacket, anchored by some neutrals, looks absolutely fabulous. And that's where black really shines. Sure it's fun to buy lively colored shoes on a whim, but we'd all go broke (and quickly run out of closet space) if we had to have a different shade of shoes to match every outfit. But there's almost nothing that black shoes and a black handbag don't go with. Conversely, a pair of bold-colored shoes will look great with any outfit from your "black is beautiful" wardrobe.

If you think of black as the foundation—rather than the defining color—of the rest of your wardrobe, you'll automatically expand the number of outfits you can create out of what you own. There doesn't have to be too much color hanging in the closet in order to make you look like you're wearing something different, and not just that same old black suit again. Don't be afraid to break up those pieces. Buying an "outfit" is great. But only wearing it that one way is not. Breaking up may be hard to do, but it's the only way to add some excitement to your wardrobe. Wear only your

What to Do When You're Ready to Make a Break

If you're a typical black-a-holic, you undoubtedly already own all the basics—a black suit (jacket and skirt), trousers, and sweater set. Now it's time to do something besides pile these black pieces on top of one another. Yes, it's time to break up the monotony. Here are a few suggestions to get you started.

- Wear the black sweater set with the khakis you have in the closet.

- Buy a sheer blouse (or sexy silk shirt) and wear it with the pants and jacket—with heels—for evening.

- Invest in another sweater set—this time, in the season's hottest color, and mix it with all of your black pieces.

- Use the black jacket to top off every other skirt you own (it's black, how could it not go?) to create new "suits."

- If you own any other jackets, try them over the black skirt and pants to make even more "suits."

→

• Wear the black pants with a brightly colored T-shirt and sneakers or loafers for the weekend.

• Add texture by topping off the black pants with a brown suede jacket or wearing the black sweater over a pair of richly colored velvet jeans.

• Don't forget about accessories. Try on a pair of red shoes or a leopard-print belt with your black pants. Or dress up the black jacket by tucking a luxurious silk or velvet scarf in a rich color or pattern inside the collar.

• Everything you mix and match doesn't have to be a solid color. Try on your black tops (the sweaters and the jacket) with any plaid, pinstriped, or printed bottoms you own. And the same works in reverse: Try topping off the black pants and skirt with striped tees, patterned sweaters, or printed blouses.

cookie-cutter, premade outfits, and you'll be constantly whining that you have nothing to wear and need to buy a new outfit. Break the outfits up, mix them, swap pieces around, and suddenly you can skip that trip to the store. You've already got a new outfit!

COLOR YOUR WORLD

I like to think that when it comes to color, perception is everything. In other words, if you treat a color as if it's a shocking invasion into your otherwise drab and monochromatic wardrobe, then it *will* stand out like a sore thumb. Every time you open your closet, you'll be taunted by that bright pink (or red or yellow or whatever) jacket that's hanging all alone and set apart from the general sea of black. I'm not going to attempt to get you to disown all your black clothing, but in order to brighten it up a bit, you need to start thinking of color as an accessory.

Women are so afraid of color—especially if they've been hiding out under the security blanket of black for several years—that they've gotten to a point where they honestly don't know how to wear it. No one seems to know anymore what goes together. Anytime I bring a customer a few pieces that

aren't in the same shade family, I inevitably get the question: "But does it go together?" And that's when I tell them what my mother (who has never been even a little bit afraid of colorful clothing) always says: "The sky is blue, the grass is green, and every flower has different hue." Her point being that somehow *they* all manage to go together. If you doubt it, just look outside and see how those various palettes get along. Nature obviously knew a thing or two about mixing shades!

Now I'm not suggesting that you run out and start buying clothes that make you look like a garden in full spring bloom, but the point is that many different colors can be successfully mixed together, whether in vibrant, kaleidoscopic combinations or as a single shade worn with a base of neutrals. And you need to rid your mind of the idea that for things to "match" they have to all be the exact same color. A customer of mine was buying a gift for her mother and had picked out a coral cashmere sweater. I found her a pair of cashmere gloves to go with the gift. Her first question was, "Will they match?" My answer was, No, they don't match. They *tone*. It's not about finding two pieces in the exact same shade, it's about putting together a harmony of shades and tones that work together. After all, as I explained to this customer, you're not wearing these things one right on top of the other. And besides, different textures and fabrics take to color differently, so it's extremely rare to find a sweater that exactly "matches" a jacket in the restrictive sense that my customer meant. Back in the forties there was a firm that actually dyed sweaters and skirts to match, but it was a look that was so sterile and dull. Isn't it much more interesting to see the subtle variances in shades?

For beginners—people who've shied away from real color for whatever reason—I always try to suggest a single piece (a sweater is a good place to start) in whatever happens to be the season's hottest accent color. For a small investment, and a small risk, you can really liven up your basic wardrobe and add a modern, even trendy, touch. The accent color should be used in your wardrobe the same way it is used in decorating your house. Injecting a new color into your wardrobe is like tossing a beautiful, vibrant new throw pillow onto your same old couch. It makes an immediate and noticeable difference, doesn't it?

The way I look at it, you can approach wearing color in one of two ways: You can either think of it as a bold accent to cheer up all your neutrals or treat the color itself as the neutral and wear it with everything else. The results are actually the same either way, it's just a difference in perception. In my opinion, every color can be treated as a neutral if you look at it that way. The word *neutral* is one that I really try to plant in people's brains. Nothing is outlandish unless you treat it that way. If a customer tells me she can't buy a red skirt because it'll stick out in her closet, since it is the only red thing she owns, I say then don't think of it as red. Treat it like a black skirt and put all your neutral tops with it.

Another example is a customer who came in looking for a jacket. I found her a great banana-colored jacket that fit her so perfectly she looked like a million dollars. But, of course, her first question was, "What can I wear this with?" Now I happen to know that she already has a closet full of basics—browns, black, navy, gray flannel—and she can wear it with any of those pieces and look smashing. How many more alternatives do you want for one little jacket? The key is to just throw the jacket on as you would a scarf. Use it as an accessory. Use it as a way to add color to all those drab neutrals.

People who do try to buy color will inevitably ask me which shades I think they should wear. It's that word *should* that bothers me. I don't think there should be any real hard-and-fast

Betty's Favorite Color Combos

Granted, I can't reach into your closet and tell you what shirt to put with what jacket, but I can share a few mixtures that always look wonderful. Some are decidedly basic, some a bit more adventuresome—the rest is up to you!

- Gray looks great with most other neutrals. Try it with black, brown, and other shades of gray. Just be sure the colors are distinct enough to complement each other without blending together and looking too muddy.

- Navy mixed with the proverbial red and a touch of white still connotes spring to me. There is something so crisp about those colors.

- Pink, coral, and peach are all very becoming to the complexion and go beautifully with navy, light gray, brown, or beige.

- Heather blue, lavender, and lilac are gorgeous in combination with lighter shades of gray as well as with brown.

rules when it comes to playing with colors. Does an artist sit down with a color chart and a rule book before putting paint on a canvas? Of course not, and neither should you when you're putting together an outfit. So when someone asks me what color they should wear, I turn the decision back to them and make them try on a variety of shades. Because the answer isn't what color I perceive them in or even what color they think they want to wear; it's the color in which they like themselves the minute they put it on and face the mirror.

I know a lot of women fell into that whole "Color Me Beautiful" thing and had their colors done. They show up at the store and pull their little Janovic Plaza paint chip charts out of their bags, holding them up to every piece of clothing before they'll even think about taking it into the dressing room and trying it on. I respect the concept, because I think it has given a lot of women the security of knowing what colors to look at when they shop, and the confidence that they'll look good in whatever they choose—provided they never stray off that color chart. But that's where I have a problem with it: The fact that once a woman has her color chart done, those same colors are imbedded in her brain (and her closet), and she is likely to never vary them. Palettes will change, the colors you see in the stores change, *Vogue* will come out every season and declare that certain colors are "in"—but the woman who's been told she is a "winter" will not try colors outside her predefined range.

Many women seem to think there are unbreakable rules that everyone must follow when it comes to wearing color (which the whole "Color Me Beautiful" system helped foster). I know redheads who won't wear red and blondes who think yellow washes them out. Then there are women with olive-toned skin who are convinced that certain shades give them a sickly appearance. And many black women refuse to wear anything that's brown. I believe that all women can wear all colors. I've always felt that way, but over the years, I've also developed likes and dislikes of my own. Don't think of these as "rules," but merely my observations and opinions.

I won't dress myself—or anyone else—in head-to-toe color. Most women don't like it, and there's really no longevity in it. Clothes are very expensive today, and when you're making that sort of investment in them you don't want to end up looking faddish. Crayola colors may be big at the moment, but I'll only do them as accents. For some reason the designers and the magazines all decide to push the same colors in any given season. And what if you don't happen to like the so-called "color of the season"? Well, that's when you really have to take the plunge and pull out the accent colors you do like. Or you can buy a sweater or a scarf or a handbag in a new shade. You have to gamble a bit with color. I don't think there's any correct procedure for wearing it.

That said, some colors do of course look better on some people over others. Most **gray-haired women** I know shy away from gray flannel colors. I tend to agree, but you can still wear grays, you just need to accent them with a flash of red or purple or yellow. I personally don't like gray right up to the face. I've never seen anyone look good in it. I find it to be too heavy an accent for most people's complexions. The gray flannel trouser will always be a wardrobe staple, but to look good in it you need to top it off with something in another shade or texture. I think you can take away a lot of the harshness by wearing a suede jacket or maybe a leather vest over a soft silk blouse. So, in other words, the right accent can be as much about mixing textures as it is about mixing colors. This same theory holds true for **black women,** whose skin brightens

- Burgundy looks very rich paired with light gray or a darker charcoal shade, but if you're really adventurous, try it with a paler, almost skin-toned pink.

- Black goes with anything of course, but some things are chicer than others. Ivory (as opposed to stark white) or navy make a subtle combination with black. Or try colors you would normally avoid—yellow, light green—and see how striking they can be as an accent to black.

How to Break the Color Code

- You don't need a high-priced "color consultant" to tell you what looks good on you.

- Go to a mirror where there's good, natural light and hold various shades up to your face. Do certain colors light up your complexion while others seem to drain the life out of it? That's a start.

- You don't need to match your clothing to your eyes or your hair, but be aware of which shades complement them and make them stand out more beautifully.

- There's nothing wrong with having a "signature color" (Diana Vreeland was known for wearing and surrounding herself with things red), but it can be just as boring to get locked into one shade as it is to wear nothing but black or neutrals.

- I've never known a woman who didn't look good in pink. I think it looks clean and sensuous on everyone (not to mention incredibly feminine).

not only when they wear luxurious, jewel-toned colors, but also in contrast to rich textures like velvet.

And by the way, the idea that **redheads** can't wear red is a myth. The reason redheads think they can't wear red is that there are a lot of ugly reds out there. In other words, the difference is all in the particular shade of red you're wearing. Show someone a coat in a subtle, deep, warm red, and they'll go to it immediately. But when you take the tone up into the very shrieky, orangey reds people will often react vehemently against it. Those shrieky colors (we used to call them neons back in the eighties, when Stephen Sprouse popularized them) are very hard for anyone to wear, and when you also have vibrant-colored hair, the overall effect can be rather blinding.

My advice is to not be so rigid in the way you think about color—or about fashion in general. Of course you'll find certain shades, certain styles, certain designers' cuts that time after time make you look and feel fabulous. Great, wear those as much as you like. But don't be afraid to go a little crazy sometimes if that makes you feel good. Pick up something, like a velvet or chiffon scarf in the "color of the season," or buy a bold-colored sweater just because it catches your eye. I've been known to wear the brightest of colors on the darkest, rainiest days, and that's simply because it makes *me* feel good. And it apparently makes other people feel good because I've been told I look sunny and cheerful to those who enter my office from the dark, dreary street below. And if I look good too, well then that's *really* something.

But don't, please don't, buy a color you *really* don't like. I've watched women put on something that I think looks fabulous, but I'm just taking an objective look at the way the whole outfit works together. But the customer may look at herself in the mirror, and something in her face changes, and she'll say, "Oh, I can't. I really hate this color." Who knows why. Maybe she has something in her head that it reminds her of. That yellow sweater could remind her of Gulden's mustard for all I know. Personally, there's never a time when I pick up orange and don't think about Halloween. It's thoroughly ingrained in my brain. It's funny how there is a color associated with every holiday. So if a color turns you off for any reason (I don't care how "in" it is), you won't wear it—so don't buy it.

• If you're really unsure about what color will go with the skirt you already own, bring a swatch with you when you shop (just take a small snip of fabric from the inside seam of the skirt).

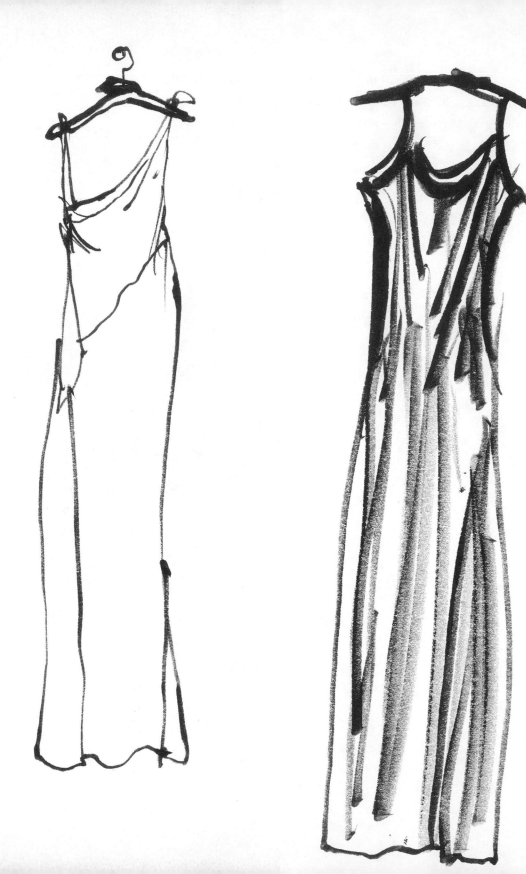

Chapter 5

STEPPING IN, STEPPING OUT

Part

1

> Who better to write a book on style than Betty, one of the chicest and best-dressed women I know! I would trust this woman with my ~~life~~—closet!
> —Joan Rivers

BIG-NIGHT JITTERS

*G*etting dressed for a special occasion probably causes women more trauma than just about anything else.

It's one of the few times when a customer comes to me and says, "I *need* a dress." And she really means it. This is no impulse buy. This is the one time when even women who normally don't care too much about clothes really labor over what to wear—shop extensively, try on compulsively, and maybe even buy (and return) by the shopping bagful. I think part of the panic is that the special occasion—whether it's a wedding, charity ball, or New Year's Eve party—is a time when we're dressing for other people. We are dressing to be seen (if you didn't want to be seen, you'd stay home). That may also be the reason that the first thing every woman says to me when she comes in looking for that special dress is, "I want to look sexy." It doesn't matter if she's eighteen or eighty, every woman wants to look sexy when she gets dressed up. But what, exactly, does *sexy* mean these days?

Sexy has suddenly become the most overused—and, I think, misused—word around. It used to just refer to what was behind the bedroom door and the look of certain Hollywood stars. Carole Lombard in her bias-cut silk blouses—now *that* was sexy. But I don't think most women even know what they mean when they say it. A woman who walks into my dressing room in pursuit of sexiness is not necessarily looking for a dress that's skintight, cut down to there, or provocative in any blatant sort of way. I think we've gotten our images—and our words—confused. I think what every woman wants, especially when she's

> We call Betty the miracle worker! Her solution to everything is personal and perfect.
> —Jean Doumanian, film producer

getting dressed up for a special occasion, is to look pretty. And to look feminine. To look, well, like a *woman*. And I suppose that is sexy on some level. It's certainly a lot sexier than the boring suit or pants-and-sweater dressing most women sport every other day of the week.

Now why is it that, regardless of how far in advance we start thinking about how sexy and pretty we want to look for the evening, everyone still waits until the last minute to actually buy a dress for a big event? It's like a disease that no one seems to be able to shake off. No matter how much time we spend fretting about it, looking through our closets, and wandering through the stores, I'd venture to say that ninety percent of women still find themselves without a dress at the eleventh hour. That all seems to be part of the fun: I'll wait till the week before, get really frantic, and then I'll find something just in the nick of time. Part of the procrastination may be linked to guilt, because on a psychological level most women don't feel comfortable about the fact that they will end up spending a lot of money on a dress they might only wear once. So then you fall into the trap of looking for a dress to wear to one specific event, but as you look you keep thinking of other possible places and events the dress could also be suitable for. That

Sheer

Solid

Bolero jackets

can be tough, but I think it is the only way to shop today. Unless you are the bride herself, you really should find a dress that can be worn many times over. Even if you will be seeing the same people at several different parties or events, you just have to keep coming up with creative new ways to package the outfit. You can wear a different accessory, or throw an elaborate scarf or a dressy bolero jacket over it to change the look completely. Keep building onto the dress as you would any other core piece in your wardrobe.

Here is just one example of how many lives a single dress can lead: I have a fabulous leopard print chiffon evening dress that I bought at least twenty-five years ago, and I just recently wore it to a wedding. It originally had a matching scarf around the neck, which I had made into a sash. I had a little padding added to the shoulders (and let it out in the areas where I'd gained weight), but it is essentially the same dress. The lesson here? Hold on to evening clothes. They are the one thing I really don't believe in giving away. You may not wear them exactly the same way years later, but a good evening dress is fixable and can be made to look new again. Sometimes a long dress can become a cocktail dress, or you can alter it in some other way to get a few more spins out of it.

When you buy an expensive evening dress (and let's face it, they *are* expensive), you've got to love it. This is not the time to settle for something and then try to make do. If you're going to wear this dress for special occasions for years to come, it should be something that every time you pull it out of the closet you think to yourself, Gee, I *really* love this dress. And since you are spending a lot of time, energy, and money in the pursuit of this one dress, you also want to try to get the best value for the price. Now that's not necessarily the same thing as getting a dress that's on sale for a bargain price. Sometimes—but

The One-Dress Evening Wardrobe

Use a simple dress, be it long or short, as your foundation and build an entire evening wardrobe around it—dressing it up or down as the occasion warrants.

- Slipping into sheer stockings and strappy, high-heeled sandals adds instant sex appeal, while more opaque hose and close-toed pumps give a serious, less dressy message.

- Use jewelry to change the look from fun (chunky bangles) to fancy (pearl earrings and a matching choker).

- Toss a cashmere shawl or cardigan over your shoulders for a classic, more casual look; a beaded or lacy bolero jacket to make the dress "black tie" appropriate.

- Change the look of the neckline by wrapping a chiffon, velvet, or silk scarf around your neck and letting the ends trail over your shoulders.

How to Take Your Suit Out on the Town

You may not be able to go from the boardroom straight to the ballroom, but here are a few easy ways to make your work clothes a little more playful.

• Don't underestimate the power of high heels. Slip on some stilettos and you will automatically look more dressed up and infinitely sexier.

• A lighter leg goes a long way—change your dark stockings for sheer ones before leaving the office.

• Leave your briefcase behind and carry just the evening's essentials in a smaller, dressier bag (if you're in a bind, a makeup case in a funky animal print or shiny satin can double as an evening clutch).

• Take your shirt off! Showing a little bare skin under a fitted suit jacket (or try just a silk camisole if the neckline is too low) gives your daytime suit more of a nighttime look.

• Bring extra accessories. Adding a bold necklace,

unfortunately, not always—buying an expensive dress really does give you a lot of value for the money. You need to be a little bit savvy to tell the difference between a well-made dress and a cheaply made one, because that difference is no longer always reflected in the price tag. Turn the dress inside out and take a good look at how it's made. You should check to see if it's lined; if the pattern lines up at the seams; how well the buttons, zippers, and hems are sewn; and make sure there aren't loose threads hanging all over. Also, if you may want to let the dress out somewhere down the line (hey, it could happen), you should hold the seams up to the light to determine whether there is any selvage. If the seam has an inch of extra fabric, that means you have a half inch that can be let out (you have to preserve enough

the one dress evening wardrobe

pearl earrings
matching choker

toss a cashm
shawl

to make the new seam). If there's an inch at every seam, you could conceivably let the dress out almost an entire size. Now, that could seriously add to the garment's longevity.

I think that maybe part of the reason women get so stressed out about dressing up is that no one has a clue anymore what is truly appropriate attire for any given event. Even the words "black tie" have become a misnomer. I don't think anyone really knows what that means these days. On the one hand, it is very liberating for everyone that the old hard-and-fast rules have fallen by the wayside, but on the other hand, it has also generated a lot of confusion. If everyone has her own idea of what "dressed up" means, then how do you know if you'll be dressed appropriately for your function? It has

dangling earrings, or a rhinestone hair clip is sometimes enough to turn an everyday black shift dress into a perfect little cocktail dress.

change by wrapping a scarf around your neck and letting the ends trail over your shoulders

happened to us all at one time or another: You walk into the cocktail party in a slinky, sequined dress only to find that all the other women seem to have come straight from the office and are still wearing business suits but with a slightly fancier top underneath the jacket. That's the risk you take in this anything-goes world! Hold your head high and feel confident that you probably stand out as the most dramatic-looking woman in the room. Of course, if you really feel you need to make excuses for your attire, mysteriously allude to the *very* fancy function you are going to later in the evening.

It used to be a given that if you got an invitation that said "black tie," you pulled out a long dress for the evening. That is no longer the protocol. In fact, most stores and designers have actually stopped using the words "cocktail dress" to describe those short, dressy little numbers and are instead referring to them as "black tie" dresses. Of course, long, formal evening clothes still exist, but I see very few women buying or wearing them anymore. I think the feeling is that you won't get enough wear out of a long evening dress in order to get your money's worth. Everyone is afraid to invest in long (unless they absolutely have to) because the fear is that you will wear it for that one event and then it will hang in the back of the closet gathering dust for years before you have another excuse to pull it out.

Now while I will admit that there are very few occasions these days that call for the sort of elaborate evening gowns I used to sell by the dozens back in the eighties, I think it can be very practical to invest a very simple, clean-lined long shift dress. It could be black (or any other color you like) and have a sexy slit up the side or the back. It could have a halter top or be backless or plunge to a deep V at the neck. But the point is, as long as it is a simple enough shape (and doesn't have any beading, sequins, or embroidery fussing it up), it will be a dress

chiffon
scarf

black
sleeveless
shift

it's
all in
how
you
wear
it!

you can put on time and time again for a variety of occasions.
You wouldn't want to wear it to, say, an afternoon wedding, but
it would look perfectly appropriate at almost any evening
wedding or cocktail party. And best of all, since it's simple, you
can easily add to it in order to continually change the look.

At the opposite end of the evening spectrum from the
long, formal dress are those not-so-dressy occasions that force
you to go directly from day to date. It could be just meeting
someone for dinner at a nice restaurant immediately after work,
a cocktail party at the office, or a party that's simply scheduled
too early to allow you time to rush home from the office in
between. Short of bringing a complete change of clothes, shoes,
and accessories with you to work, how can you make this
transition? Well, unless you are attending a black tie, or similarly
formal, event (for that you really have no choice but to lug a
garment bag to the office), it just takes a little clever clothes play
and a few minutes at the ladies' room mirror to get you ready.

As is often the case, black really is the best choice for
these tricky situations. It inevitably looks dressier than any
other color. It can be made to look sexy without too much
trouble. And, maybe the best reason of all, if you spill
something on yourself at lunch, chances are you can still go
straight to the party after work and no one will ever know. If
you own a sleeveless black shift with a matching jacket, wear
that. At the office you can keep the jacket on and look like
you're wearing a suit, and changing for the party can be as
simple as doffing your jacket. The same principle works with
any black suit—whether the bottom is pants or a long or short
skirt. Just don't forget to bring some extra makeup with you to
work that day. There's still something to be said for the power
of a little sultry red lipstick when you want to look dressed up.

Part 2

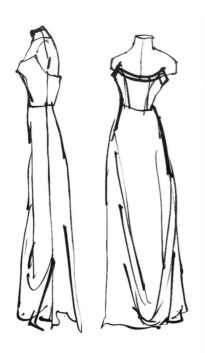

DOWN THE AISLE

There are few productions—from a Broadway spectacle to an inaugural ball—that can rival a wedding when it comes to planning, excitement, chaos, and nerves. It all begins as much as a year or more in advance, with selecting a place to hold the big event, finding a caterer, band, florist, photographer, and, of course, clothing for everyone involved. And that's usually where things start to get *really* complicated, because this is one day when all the stops are pulled, often exorbitant amounts of money are spent, and everyone who is part of the wedding is determined to look his or her best. Oh, and one more thing: They all have to get the approval of the bride before making any dressing decisions. To use a political analogy, it's like the House and the president—everyone may have a voice and even a vote, but it's the president (or, in this case, the bride) who holds the ultimate veto power.

THE MOTHER MATTER

Somehow in the midst of this flurry of activity, nerves, and excitement, everything does manage to get done, and everyone always looks wonderful. Dresses aside, I really do think that everyone's face radiates happiness on the big day, which makes them look truly beautiful. But since no one wants to rely solely on emotion to make them look good, more angst probably goes into dress choices than goes into all of the other parts of the wedding combined. And often, one of the most angst-ridden of all is the mother of the bride (also, to a somewhat lesser degree, the mother of the groom). Without exception, every mother of the bride or groom enters my office with the same line: "I *don't* want to look like the mother of the bride/groom." There is an incredibly negative stereotype wrapped up in that phrase, and usually the image that comes to

Mother of the bride

Wedding Rules for Moms

• Don't buy a dress too far ahead of time. You don't want it to look out of fashion by the time you walk down the aisle.

• Do check with your daughter or future daughter-in-law before you buy to see if she has a specific color or style in mind to help you blend in with the wedding party.

• Provided you get the bride's okay, black and off-white are no longer considered off-limits.

• Do think about your own comfort. There's no better way to make yourself miserable on the big day than by having to wear a dress that binds or shoes that give you blisters.

• Do give yourself a mini dress rehearsal—complete with shoes, hose, jewelry, and a handbag—while there's still time to fix anything that's not perfect.

mind is one of a dowdy middle-aged matron in a fussy—and inevitably, unflattering—pastel-colored, floor-length confection.

Fortunately, most of those old mandates about color, length, and style no longer hold true. Mothers of the bride and groom are pretty much free to wear whatever they like (subject to bridal approval, of course) without worrying about whether or not they match what the other side or the bridesmaids or whoever are wearing, although some of the clashing displays I have seen at weddings recently almost make me wish for some of those rules to come back into fashion. I've also witnessed weddings with a complete absence of color—snowball-like all-white affairs or mothers and attendants all in their favorite chic black.

Now that mothers of the bride and groom have shed their dowdy look in favor of something more fashionable and more individual, I think these women actually have an even harder time making a decision. There are too many choices, too many concerns, and they are plagued by the thought each time they face the mirror of the too many eyes that will be on them come the big day. I've seen mothers who shop for their dresses (and buy and return) even longer and harder and more indecisively than the brides themselves. My advice is to try to remove yourself from the fray as much as possible. Of course you'll want your daughter's or future daughter-in-law's opinion, and you want her to like and approve of whatever you choose, but don't let her bully you into something you won't feel comfortable wearing.

Depending on how fancy the wedding will be, you should think about your dress just as you would a dress for a similarly dressy special occasion, and don't let your role as mother of the bride or groom throw you into a complete tailspin. You can look through bridal magazines for ideas, but don't feel limited to dresses that are specifically labeled "mother of the bride" dresses. I think one of the biggest favors you can do for yourself is to find a helpful, knowledgeable, and sympathetic sales associate who understands weddings and can be there to guide you through the selection process, alterations, accessories, and even provide a few pats on the back. Granted, such gems are few and far between in stores today, but that's where smaller boutiques and even the local bridal shops can win out over the bigger stores.

PRETTY MAIDS ALL IN A ROW

It's always flattering to be asked to serve as a bridesmaid in a friend's or relative's wedding. Unfortunately, the flattery often ends there. Few things inspire as much fear and loathing as the bridesmaid dress. The very phrase conjures up nightmare visions of unbecoming, overpriced, and overdone concoctions of tulle, chintz, velvet, or worse. Part of the problem is availability; few top manufacturers are willing to get involved in the bridesmaid market, so choices are notoriously lacking. Another concern is trying to dress several different figure types in the same outfit: What looks lovely on your tall, willowy friend might be a disaster on your shorter, more voluptuous sister. And the final, and perhaps overriding, concern is cost. No one wants to spend an excessive amount on a dress they'll wear once for a matter of hours, and anyone who has a closet filled with past bridesmaid dresses knows that very few (if any) of them really can be worn again for another occasion. This last problem really can be offset by the bride: Shouldn't these bridesmaid dresses be part of the wedding budget? I do think

Bridesmaids

they can be shared in price (even if it's just a small percentage of the cost) by the bride.

Here is what I do when a bride first comes to me asking for help with bridesmaids' dresses, and although it's not necessarily the ultimate solution, it's a good way to start even if you are doing it on your own. The bride and I go shopping everywhere in the store, including the markdown racks, to find any dresses she likes in the color or pattern that she wants. It's an especially good idea to scour the sale racks (preferably with a helpful sales associate who knows how much stock is available and in what sizes). And since there is normally plenty of time when it comes to bridal shopping, you can often wait for the second markdown to see if the dresses you like become truly affordable. I really do advise doing a little pre-shopping without your bridesmaids in tow. It will be less confusing and less stressful in the long run if you pick out a few dresses and narrow down the choices before bringing in a chorus of naysayers.

One solution to the problem of fitting several figures into the same dress is to drop the traditional approach of trying to stuff everyone into one mold. More and more brides are breaking away from the cookie-cutter approach to bridesmaid dresses and allowing their attendants to pick their own dresses. Usually the bride will dictate a color (for obvious reasons, this works extremely well when the selected color is black), and then the bridesmaids are free to select a dress that flatters them, but still mixes with the others to present a uniform picture. It helps to coordinate the accessories, so that all of the bridesmaids wear the same (or very similar) shoes, hair ornaments, and jewelry. You can take the simplest of dresses—say, a little sleeveless shift—and dress it up with lace gloves, pearls and pearl earrings, and suddenly your bridesmaids look very similar and very beautiful.

HERE COMES
THE BRIDE

Y ou recognize her because she's usually the one in
white. The one with a veil on and a large
bouquet of flowers. She is the woman who is
the star of the big event, the princess for a day—otherwise
known as the bride. The most exciting thing to me is to see a
woman trying on the first wedding dress. Whether it's one she
really likes or not, a certain look comes over her face as she sees
herself dressed as a bride, and the reality of the whole thing
hits her, that is indescribable. Even when I've been working
with actresses who are trying on the dresses for a role, it is
always the same wonderful expression of excitement. But
that is only the beginning.

The excitement normally turns quickly into
panic and indecision, because nearly every bride
I've ever known has tried on every wedding

dress she can get her hands on before she finally makes her selection. Along the way, she'll bring in an entourage of second opinions—her mother, her best friend, bridesmaids, sometimes even the mother-in-law-to-be—anyone who can confirm how beautiful she looks. I'll wager that there isn't a single woman out there who walks into a bridal department and buys the first dress she tries on. There's a certain excitement attached just to trying on all the different dresses. Maybe it's because, theoretically, it's a once-in-a-lifetime experience. Buying a wedding dress isn't like buying any other piece of clothing. It's the one thing you never even try on until it's time. There's a huge buildup to this one event.

I think part of the thrill comes from the romance of the day. Being a bride is about as close to fairy tale land as any of us will ever get. That might help explain why so many women fall for those big, flouncy, traditional wedding dresses that are about as far as you can imagine from anything they would normally wear. I can't tell you how many times a sophisticated, well-dressed young woman has come in and told me she wants to wear something simple and chic for her wedding. Before you know it, she's tried on some enormous, romantic, flouncy dress and fallen madly in love with it. It's called fantasy—and this really is your one big chance to make it come true.

Now if you are planning to order a wedding dress, you really do have to allow yourself plenty of time. It generally takes four to six months to get a dress from the time you place the order, and even once it has arrived, you should count on several fittings and countless last-minute adjustments and changes of heart. After selecting a dress, you will also need to start thinking about the veil and headpiece, shoes, lingerie, jewelry, and your hairstyle. When you list all of the things you need to consider before being dressed to walk down the aisle, it's perfectly understandable that many brides seem to get a little neurotic as the big day draws near. But, as with everything, careful planning and careful shopping can alleviate nearly all of the last-minute anxiety.

The first fitting is when the real excitement, and the real panic, sets in. At this point it has probably been several months since you last saw the dress, and once you get it on there may be many things that aren't as you remember or suddenly aren't to your liking. Relax. You would be amazed at how many alterations and transformations can be performed on a wedding dress even up to the last minute. I have seen more tears and more promises of "I'll lose five pounds by the next fitting" at these events than I care to remember. The key is to keep a cool head and realize that almost anything is fixable. If the dress suddenly looks too plain, more lace, pearls, or other embellishments can be added. If it already looks *too* embellished, things can be removed. You can pile on extra petticoats if you think the skirt needs to look fuller. Padding can be sewn in to give you a little extra lift at the shoulders or bosom. In other words, you name it, it can probably be changed.

Most wedding dresses call for a strapless bra that goes down to the waist (like a merry widow) and possibly a petticoat, which serve as the foundation over which the dress can be fitted. And boy do I mean fitted. These things are usually pulled in so tight that there is no give whatsoever in the bodice. In other words, the dress won't go anywhere when you try to lift your arms, so you'll find you won't be able to lift them very high. The traditional wedding dress shape features the V at the

waist both in front and back upon which the whole dress is anchored. This style gives you the look of having an infinitesimal waist—and the tight fit promises to make your body look the best it's ever looked. And make you feel the most glamorous.

With dresses for any other occasion there are specific fabrics, colors, and styles that dictate when and where it can be worn. That's not so much the case with wedding dresses—at least not anymore. Except for the slinky, straight, forties-style dresses we're seeing now (which, to me, seem suited mostly to a very chic evening wedding in the city), anything really does go. I don't see much difference between what women wear for a noon wedding or an evening one. There really is no casual look when it comes to traditional wedding dresses. Chances are, if you're going to get dressed as a bride, you're going to go all out regardless of the time of day, season, or location of the wedding. And why shouldn't you?

Even for first weddings, more and more women are opting out of wearing pure white. There are so many shadings of off-white now— from ivory, ecru, and beige to soft, almost pastel shades of peach, blush, and dove gray—all of which work regardless of the season or time of day of the wedding. The only thing that really sets evening wedding dresses apart from daytime ones is the addition of glitter. When even the simplest dress is studded with little stones or beading, the light glistens off of it and the effect is spectacular. Certain fabrics do connote particular seasons—light gossamer fabrics like tulle, net, and organza are mainly reserved for summer—but many brides like the look of the heavier, more rigid silk satin and silk shantung all year round.

Next in line of importance after the dress is the veil. I like to think of the veil as the frosting on the cake, because it really does finish off the whole picture beautifully. There are as many headpiece options as there are different types of brides, so don't feel compelled to go the purely traditional route. Hats can work well for an outdoor summertime wedding, and even a simple spray of fresh flowers tucked in a neat French twist can be enough to top off a simple, sophisticated dress. The veil is also a good place to add a sentimental touch to your wedding ensemble. Even if your mother's or grandmother's dress is too old-fashioned looking or not to your taste, chances are that their veils could be remade to suit your style and complement your dress. If you are having your wedding ceremony in a church or anywhere else that involves walking down a long aisle, I really think that a dress with a train and a long veil (or at least just the long veil) are in order. It's such a dramatic way to make an entrance. And just as skirts with long trains can be bustled up to allow you to move and dance freely at the reception, long veils can be detached after the ceremony, usually leaving just the more manageable shoulder- or waist-length layer behind.

When selecting and trying on dresses and veils, it's extremely important to keep an eye on your back. A wedding ceremony is probably the one time when people actually see the back of you more than they do the front. The guests barely see the front of you until you arrive at the reception. So at each fitting, be sure to study the back of your dress, your veil, and

your hair in the three-way mirror—with your headpiece on and the train extended to its full length. You want to make sure you know exactly how you will look with your back to everyone during the ceremony.

Today, anything goes as far as the bridal shoe. The basic, classic wedding pump is a simple, low-heeled silk shoe (in a shade to match the dress), often with a small flower or bow at the front. But from there, the possibilities are endless. I've seen brides in sleek little dresses with strappy high-heeled sandals. Some brides wear sensible flats because they are afraid of tripping down the aisle. And I even know one young woman who had problem feet and was determined to be comfortable and able to dance for hours on her wedding day, so she wore white Peter Fox boots under her otherwise very traditional dress. The fact of the matter is, if you do have on a long, full dress, very few people will actually be able to see your shoes, so you might as well buy ones that feel good on your feet.

WHAT TO DO WHEN THE HONEYMOON'S OVER

After all you went through to find the perfect dress, you want to make darn sure it stays just as beautiful for years to come. And preserving your dress (perhaps your sister or your daughter or a niece will wear it someday) takes more than simply tossing it on a hanger and jamming it into the back of your closet. Unless the dress is badly stained, there usually is no need to get the dress dry-cleaned before storing it. The better (and decidedly cheaper) thing to do is to get a big box (the one the dress was shipped in is perfect), layer it with white tissue paper, stuff the sleeves with tissue paper, and layer more under the skirt. If you've stuffed it correctly, it should look like there is a body inside the dress when you're finished. Fold the dress carefully into the box and seal it with strong tape on all sides. And even more important than how you store the dress is where you store it. Warmth and dampness will discolor the fabrics and make them even more fragile. So be sure that wherever you store the dress is a generally cool, dry place.

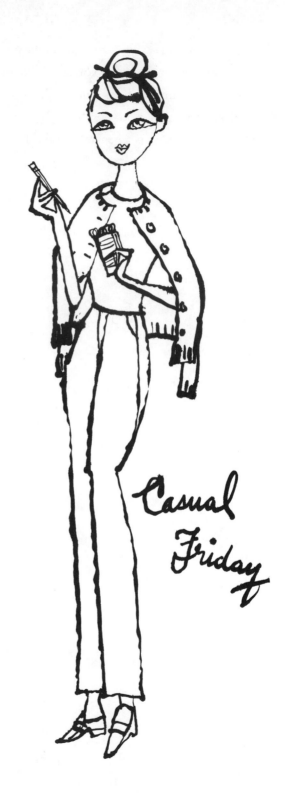

Casual
Friday

Chapter 6

THE DRESSING-DOWN DILEMMA

Part

1

The Do's and Don'ts of Dressing Down

- Do remember that even casual clothes can (and should) look neat.

- Don't just pick up whatever is on the chair next to the bed and put it back on.

- Do be sure to check your rear view.

- Don't wear leggings (or anything else) that show off your panty lines.

- Do think about accessories—like a sportier watch or some chunky link bracelets.

- Don't think that just putting on your mud-stained sneakers makes a tailored pantsuit look casual.

- Do tone down your hair and makeup to match the casual

WHAT *IS* CASUAL FRIDAY?

Back in the seventies, when women first started entering (or reentering) the workforce in droves, they came up with the most obvious solution to the problem of how to dress for their new office roles. They simply copied what men had been wearing to work for generations: the suit, oxford shirt, and necktie. The only difference was that instead of trousers, women wore dowdy, just-below-the-knee-length skirts. This was probably fashion's most unattractive moment (a moment which, unfortunately, lasted well into the eighties). These women in their shapeless, sexless navy suits and ridiculous little foulard-print ties looked more like a bunch of airline stewardesses than high-powered business executives. And worst of all, they certainly didn't look like women. How quickly we evolved from there to the current nearly-everything-goes attitude prevalent in so many offices today.

A recent survey of workplaces showed that an astonishing nine out of ten companies in the United States now allow their employees to dress down at least one day a week. With statistics like these, it's no wonder that many women (and probably some men too) are baffled when their company announces that the office is changing to casual dress either on Fridays or, in some cases, for every day of the week. For years you've been building up a wardrobe of suits which, while sometimes rather boring, at least always made you feel appropriately dressed for any business situation. But suddenly that old wisdom has been thrown out and you're given the freedom to dress more casually. The new rules leave many wondering, What's appropriate? Can I really go to a board meeting or client luncheon wearing a T-shirt and khakis? What will the others be wearing? While the business suit sort of leveled the playing field and put everyone

style (use natural-looking lipstick instead of blood red).

• **DON'T** opt for a naked face and unwashed hair tucked under a baseball cap.

Casual Yet Neat

Here are a few looks that are guaranteed not to get you demoted.

- Never underestimate the power of a basic blazer. Toss a classic black or navy jacket on—even over simple blue jeans and a white T-shirt—and suddenly you look more professional.

- Wear denim in pieces besides jeans. A crisp, unfaded denim shirt can bring a black pantsuit down to a more casual level.

- Jackets that aren't really jackets—like an unconstructed, long knit cardigan—can soften up your look without losing respectability.

- T-shirt style dresses (so long as they're not too short or too clingy) can be the perfect casual day solution. Dress it up slightly by tossing a jacket or cardigan on top.

in the same state of dress (just as wearing a uniform does for children at school), the flexibility of casual office dressing leaves an awful lot up to the discretion of the individual. While one may take *casual* to mean shorts and a T-shirt, another might decide on an unconstructed pantsuit. Now won't they both feel slightly awkward and out of place when they come together for a business meeting?

When you think of dressed-down office attire, Armani probably isn't the first thing that comes to mind, but his clothes were really the forerunner of this whole craze. He took the concept from a high-fashion point of view with his impeccably tailored pantsuits, but the trickle-down effect was nearly immediate. As soon as Armani made it fashionable and acceptably chic for women to wear pants for business and parties, designers and manufacturers at every price and style level followed suit. And now everyone just goes to the Gap and gets the same look. But casual is not new—just look at Katharine Hepburn. She made trousers and men's shirts look sexy and chic decades and decades ago. The difference is that back then she was wearing them as a mark of her own personal style. Now we do it to look like everyone else!

I think the most important rule to keep in mind is that casual doesn't mean sloppy. You can dress in casual attire, and yet still look completely polished and pulled together (a little makeup and well-groomed hair helps). And in that case, you will still feel appropriate in a business setting. The other problem comes when people mistake casual attire for overly sexy clothing. While a cropped sweater or halter top looks great on the weekend, that sort of overexposure is never acceptable in an office situation. If you do work in an office that has gone the way of casual dressing, take your fashion cues from your coworkers. I'm not normally a big advocate of fashion conformity, but the workplace is one instance where the word *appropriate* still resonates. The definitions of dressing for success may have changed radically since the navy suit and bow tie days, but appearance does still count for something in the professional world. A safe bet is to look to your superiors at work and see what they are wearing. I'm certainly not suggesting that you copy their wardrobes piece for piece, but if, for example, your boss always wears neat trousers and a sweater set or nice shirt on "casual day," then you should think twice about ever wearing shorts or jeans to the office.

Another business trend that is having its impact on the fashion world is the fact that more and more people are moving their offices into their homes. If it's okay to wear what used to be your play clothes to the office, then what on earth are these work-at-home types dressing in? I think it's very easy to fall into a bad habit of never getting yourself dressed—sitting around your home office in your robe or sweat suit all day. At the very least, I say try to be sure you dress in something different every day. Don't just grab the same sweatshirt and leggings you pulled off the night before. There is certainly no need to put on a suit, stockings, and pumps, but stand in front of the mirror and put on something presentable. The trap that so many women fall into is in thinking, Who's going to see me? And soon you aren't only sitting around your home office looking a mess, you're out running errands, meeting people for lunch, and perhaps accidentally bumping into business associates. So even if you only dress for yourself, the rest of the world really will appreciate it.

casual but neat

... never underestimate the power of a basic blazer

Part 2

GIVE ME A "T"

*I*t seems to me that the whole concept of dressing down started with the evolution of the T-shirt.

There were golf shirts and polo shirts (which women stole from men's dressers for weekend wear), but the true T-shirt was originally confined to a man's underwear drawer. Gradually these men's staples made their way out from under and became a necessity for men, women, and children alike. The classic Gap pocket tee was at the forefront of the trend, back when T-shirt dressing still called for big and baggy. But now it seems that women's tees shrink down to tinier and tighter versions each season. Some are positively microscopic!

It's hard to find a single item of clothing that has become as versatile, acceptable, and omnipresent as the T-shirt. You see them under Armani suits at the office (on both men and women), at the gym, with jeans, and emblazoned with every logo and saying you can think of. I find myself practically standing on my head sometimes trying to read everyone's chests and backs while I walk down the street. It makes sense to build an entire wardrobe of T-shirts, especially since the style has been co-opted by fashion designers who turn out versions not just in the traditional cotton, but also in velvet, satin, silk, and even cashmere. With all this variety to choose from, who really needs any other sorts of tops at all? During the summer months, the T-shirt even grows into a versatile little dress. And the interesting thing is that the T-shirt truly is fashion for the masses. Since you can find them at every price—from the three-for-$10 variety up to designer versions

costing hundreds of dollars—it is one look that truly is available to everyone. And you certainly don't have to spend lavishly to dress well in them. A fine cotton tee that's kept in good condition (yes, they do look better when they're ironed) sits just as well under a jacket as the pricier versions.

Casual, especially as it relates to a work wardrobe, usually means pants to most women. And it is a great freedom to be able to wear them to the office—more comfortable for sitting at the desk, easier for driving to work, and less cumbersome for running around the office from meeting to meeting. Maybe men really have known best all along. There are so many options and styles all born out of that basic two-legged design—wide, narrow, stretch, pleated, flat-front, etc.—that many women get put off trying to choose. But I say the answer is simple: Wear what is becoming on you. You can take fashion into account (generally one style or another is proclaimed as the "pant of the season"), but in the end you'll only wind up looking silly unless you stick with the style that suits your figure best. Pants can be particularly hard to fit, so I'm also a firm believer in buying more than one pair if you find something that truly fits and flatters you. They don't really go out of style, but they might not still be offered next time you're in the market. I know. I've learned this lesson the hard way.

When dressing gets more laid back, it all but eliminates the age syndrome. Suddenly everyone from toddlers to grandmothers is able to dress in the same styles. Just take a look at Baby Gap—all those shrunken-down versions of their parents' jeans, T-shirts, and khaki pants. It's the great equalizer—crossing all the barriers from age to financial situation. Let's take jeans, for example. Would the farmer of long ago ever believe that we'd all be walking around in his work clothes? Not to mention the prices we're willing to pay for them. Now that jeans—much like T-shirts—come in every imaginable color and fabric, they've become completely acceptable as "real" pants. Black stretch jeans often find their way to the office paired up with a jacket to create a comfortable, casual kind of makeshift suit. And velvet or stretch satin versions show up at holiday parties paired with silk blouses, T-shirts, or soft sweaters.

Technology—in the form of comfortable new stretch fabrics—has made relaxed dressing a lot better looking in recent years. It's easier now to buy clothes that fit well and allow you to trim yourself down or show off an already thin, fit figure. Don't hide behind casual—wearing baggy, oversized clothes or your husband's castoffs in the name of relaxed dressing. Take the ubiquitous leggings, for example, and see how much more flattering they can be than a huge pair of sweat pants. The solution for the not-so-perfect figure is to top off slim pants or leggings with a longer sweater, jacket, shirt, or T-shirt to create an illusion of slimness.

Stretch is being added to everything—pants, shirts, skirts, jackets—and to every fabric. You can find stretchy spandex and Lycra woven into cotton, denim, velvet, even wool jerseys. The key to wearing stretch clothes is to find a good fit, and it has nothing to do with price level. You simply have to try on—a lot. I think some of the best stuff comes from the Gap. And since I tend to doubt how long some of these things will last, why not buy them at a price that makes them fun to wear and at which you don't have to feel married to them. If at the end of the season, your $40 stretch pants bag at the knees—elastic does break down in cleaning—then okay. But, for longevity's sake, you should at least try to avoid tossing these fabrics in the dryer because the heat really does a job on that elastic.

I think stretch fabrics have a really nice feeling to them,

though for some it may take a bit of getting used to. A heavier woman can look very svelte in them—once she's struggled into them—because they hold you in. It's like getting into a bed that's made very tightly. These aren't clothes for people who'd rather kick off all the covers. But stretch does expand and contract with you and, after you've worn it a few times, it will sort of contour and mold to your body.

JOIN THE SWEATER SET

I honestly don't think there is a chapter big enough to cover all there is to say about sweaters. I could fill a whole book on this topic alone. They are basic, yet extremely fashionable. They stay home, go to the office, and out to dinner. They can look dressed down or dressed to kill. Sweaters even show up at black tie events. What other item of clothing can possibly do all of these things? I know women who are absolute sweater freaks. They will buy unique sweaters at any price to add to their vast collections. To them, sweaters are not just pieces of clothing—they are collectibles, like china or dolls.

The most obvious place to begin building your sweater wardrobe is with a simple style pullover in a basic shade—like black. It can be a crewneck, turtleneck, V neck, jewel neck, or whatever you like best, and can be knit out of anything from

cotton to merino wool to silk or cashmere. You'll wear it with trousers, skirts, jeans, alone, or under a jacket. I guarantee you will pull that sweater out of your drawer more often than anything else you own. Add a cardigan over it and you have a sweater set that will expand your wardrobe options even further. Not only can they be worn together, but the cardigan can replace a jacket, or you can toss it over your shoulders all year round, keeping it handy for any time you get too cool. When it comes to the amount of use and versatility you get for your investment, the sweater set has really become as much of a necessity as the proverbial little black dress.

My advice would be to buy whatever is the most luxurious-feeling sweater you can afford. I think it is every woman's dream to own a cashmere sweater, whether she is buying the most luxurious, expensive one or outlet store bargains. And those cashmere sweaters will never go out of style, so they really are a fantastic investment. All the more reason to protect them. Get out those mothballs as soon as the winter is over. I hear about so many people whose storage areas and closets are infested with moths and field mice. I've always thought those animals must have beautiful nests, all lined in different colors of cashmere sweaters. The mice probably have nicer sweaters than I do.

There are differences in cashmere, and not all of it has the same buttery feel and incredible longevity. I know women my age who still proudly own cashmere sweaters from their college days that are still in perfect condition. But there are just as many sweaters (even expensive ones) that start to pill and lose their shape after just a few seasons. If you are knowledgeable, you can feel the difference with your hand. It has to do with the quality of the wool and how pure it is, not necessarily with the weight of the yarn. The best cashmere is typically that which is imported from Scotland. When you compare it to, say, cashmere from China, you'll notice that the one from China seems to have another type of hair in it—probably angora—which gives it an itchier feel against your skin. Unfortunately, many manufacturers don't divulge the wool's origin on the label, so you are left to trust your own sense of touch. You can find cashmere sweaters in two-ply or four-ply, but that doesn't mean better or worse—just lighter and heavier. Some people find the heavier, pure cashmeres too smothering; some may be allergic. In that case, try on a silk and cashmere blend or a fine merino wool. Both have a luxurious feeling that's similar to cashmere and are usually very durable.

While it is one thing to try to judge the quality of a sweater by feel, I'm afraid you'll have to go one step further and actually take it to the dressing room in order to figure out whether or not the sweater really fits you. I can't tell you how many women I see walking to the cash register with sweaters they grabbed off the shelf and didn't bother to try on. That is a big mistake, because all sweaters are certainly not created equal. Until you put it on, there is really no way to judge the size, the length of the sleeves, the positioning of the neckline, or where it will

Six Uses for a Sweater Set

1. Tie the cardigan around your waist anytime you're wearing a dress that you think reveals more of your tummy and backside than you'd like it to.

2. Wrap the sleeves of the cardigan, scarflike, around your neck when the wind picks up.

3. Try the crewneck on under a sleeveless dress to create an instant jumper.

4. Slip the crewneck on over a sleeveless or short-sleeve dress to create a sweater and skirt combination.

fall in relation to your waist or hips. If you have a large bosom, you should not even bother trying on any cropped sweaters because chances are they will leave you looking rather top-heavy. And every woman—I don't care how good her figure is—should be wary of those long sweaters with the binding around the bottom. That binding is the kiss of death for most sweaters because it hits you in exactly the wrong place. That's what I call a real hip-hugger, and it's the kind you don't want. If you are trying to conceal a not-so-perfect figure, look for a long, slim sweater that falls *below* your hips and is not bound at the bottom. When you slip it on over a straight skirt or slim pants you are able to create a long, svelte look. It's a very good way to cloak a figure that is a bit chunky on top, but slim on the bottom. Cashmere is ideal for concealing a tummy or hips because the wool has enough body of its own to not cling to your body. Some of the silks, cottons, and chenille knits will cling to every lump, bump, and bulge.

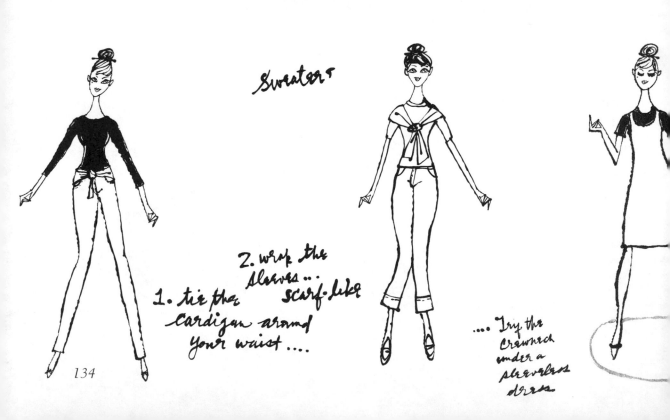

Sweaters

1. tie the cardigan around your waist ....

2. wrap the sleeves ... scarf-like

.... Try the crewneck under a sleeveless dress

Although sweaters have never exactly gone out of style, I can't help but think the current resurgence of the twin set is a direct result of the slimming down of fashion. Designers started cutting jackets so close to the body that a few seasons back Karl Lagerfeld actually had to create special corsets to be worn under his Chanel jackets. Now, with or without the Scarlett O'Hara–type underpinnings, many women—the type with real bodies and real bosoms and real desks to sit at all day—simply could not squash themselves into such tight-fitting jackets. Nor did many of them even want to try. So what is the working woman to do if she doesn't want to wear a jacket? The answer, of course, came in the form of the sweater set. The cardigan—especially a long, slim, shapely one—is an excellent and completely acceptable alternative to a jacket at the office. Try breaking up your twin sets and mixing and matching each piece with other parts of your wardrobe. The crewneck

5. Wear the cardigan alone with several buttons undone . . . sexy!

6. Pair one or both pieces with a slinky satin or crushed velvet skirt for a holiday cocktail party.

4. .....wear the cardigan alone, unbuttoned

... Slip the crewneck on OVER a Sleeveless dress ...

5.

6. ... pair one or both pieces with a slinky satin ... skirt

can go under a jacket or over a blouse. The cardigan can be worn alone all buttoned up, over just about any sort of blouse or T-shirt, under a jacket or in place of one, or you can even nip it in at the waist with a thin leather belt. And as long as you're mixing things up, don't forget to experiment a bit with color. After all, how can you go wrong by buying a sweater in a favorite color?

Back in the fifties we had the most beautiful and luxurious evening sweaters. They were usually cashmere, and they were covered with beading, elaborate embroidery, pearls, or sequins. Now you will often see these same sweaters turning up at thrift stores and vintage clothing booths at antique shows and flea markets. If you are tempted to buy one (and who wouldn't be?), be sure to check it over carefully before you make a purchase. One that seems to be a bargain but is missing some beadwork or has holes in the embroidery may not be such a bargain once you find out how incredibly expensive it is to fix that sort of handwork. In lieu of the authentic evening sweater, be creative in wearing the sweaters you already own for dressier occasions. By simply adding a pearl choker or chunky silver or gold chain to a plain, fitted, crew, or V-neck sweater you can often dress it up enough to pair with a long evening skirt or short, sexy mini for a dinner party.

And don't stop your sweater collection with the traditional tops. Sweater dressing can extend from head to toe with skirts, dresses, pants, and coats all knit from the same wonderfully cozy yarns. If you are happiest in your unconstructed running suit, then invest in a cashmere "sweat suit," for the same level of comfort but with *much* more appeal. The only problem with sweatery pants and skirts is that they do tend to get baggy. Cleaning will help get them back, but the only true solution—and it's an expensive one—is to get them reblocked.

Chapter

THE
INSIDE
STORY

Part

1

FASHION IS
ONLY SKIN DEEP

*Y*ears ago I did a lot of work with the wardrobe people who dressed all of the big soap opera stars. They would buy plenty of extravagant evening gowns and dressy suits, but all in all I think I sold them more lingerie than I did clothing. We would scour the lingerie department together, and they would snap up every provocative gown, robe, teddy, and camisole they could get their hands on. That was, of course, before the days when everyone began to appear nearly nude on these shows. The fact that not even our fantasy characters are indulging in pretty lingerie is, for me anyway, a rather depressing trend. There has been a general movement away from recognizing the importance, the provocative appeal, and the necessity of beautiful, sexy, well-made lingerie and sleepwear.

Deep down, however, I can't help but think that lingerie is going to make its comeback, if for no other reason than the fact that it is so beautiful. With everyone dressing so casually and concerned with getting more value for the money they spend on their wardrobes, lingerie is, quite naturally, no longer a top concern. In fact, anytime someone has a limited amount set aside for clothing, expensive lingerie is the first budget-cutting casualty. Okay, even I have to admit that you don't *need* fancy, pricey underthings, but they *are* fun. I mean if you're not ever going to wear a fancy evening dress, how about slipping into a beautiful silk nightgown once in a while?

Lingerie—and certainly luxurious negligees—has in some ways become obsolete in our hurry-up workaday world. People just decided that it was the one thing they wouldn't waste their time and money on. We put all our effort and our wallets into our outer packaging. Most women, especially, put an awful lot of time and money into taking care of the outside details—

from clothes to hair, makeup, and nails—but so little care and thought go into our most intimate attire. It never ceases to amaze me that women exist who won't bat an eyelash over spending a few thousand dollars on a designer suit, but who will balk at a trip to the lingerie department for a $40 bra. These women will peel off their expensive outerwear only to reveal bras and panties that are literally in tatters. I swear some of them have been wearing the same bra since the seventies. And I don't care how good or how expensive that bra was when you bought it, they simply aren't built to last anywhere near that long. You can only hike that elastic up so high before you just have to bite the bullet and buy some new underwear.

Why shouldn't you wear pretty underwear? After all, it is what you put on first every day, setting the tone in some way for your exterior layers. Everything else is really just

newsflash:
woman hit
by bus in old underwear

covering. And not only is it nice to have pretty underwear on under your clothes, but you never know when you may be glad it's there! I can't tell you how many times customers have gotten dressed in front of me and excused themselves for the underwear they had on—or didn't have on, as is often the case. I always say to them, Don't be silly, you're no different than anyone else. But then when a woman does go into my dressing room and she's wearing beautiful underwear, you can be certain she's not going to be making any excuses.

I can remember going shopping with my mother as a little girl. You always had to have on your best underwear—God forbid the salesperson at the store might catch a glimpse of you not in your newest, best, unfaded, cleanest underwear. It's like the old cliché about wearing clean underwear because you never know when you might get hit by a bus. Well, I have to say that I have never seen a picture in the newspaper of some poor soul with her skirt up over her head and everyone examining her underwear, yet it still seems to be every mother's nightmare.

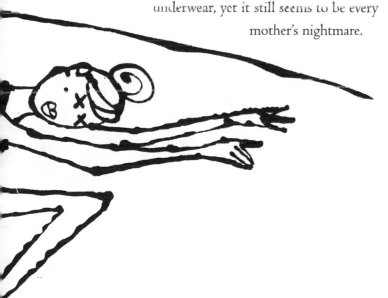

Part 2

IF THE BRA FITS . . .

We've come a long way since the bra-burning, let-it-all-hang-out days of the sixties and seventies. And it seems that since then women have divided themselves into two camps: the ones who will wear any old thing, no matter how tattered, under their expensive outer clothes; and the ones who can't resist the allure of something a little feminine and frilly next to their skin. It is that second group who go berserk for Wonderbras and other padded extravagances. There were women lined up outside of department stores all over this country when that Wonderbra was first introduced. I guess whenever breasts come back into fashion (and they always do), so does the elaborate bra, because, at any price, it's still a lot cheaper than the surgical alternative.

I'm always surprised to find, in the midst of so much budget-consciousness, that there still is a large group of women

who are willing to spend lavishly on their bras. I had a customer say to me the other day, "I must be crazy. I bought a bra for $85—and now I'm here to buy some more!" And stores like Victoria's Secret certainly would not do such big business if women weren't interested in curvy, lacy, even downright fussy, bras and matching panties. And I really don't think this is just a male admiration thing. I mean I'm not in their bedrooms so I don't know what's going on, but I really think these feminine underthings are purchased to boost a woman's own self-esteem. And why not? There's no better feeling than having a silk bra or camisole against your skin even when outwardly your dress is all business.

So many women have a problem with bras because of poor fit. There's nothing more uncomfortable—or unattractive under your clothing—than an ill-fitting bra. And I think the

A huge percentage of women are actually walking around in the wrong size bra—and every time they go shopping, for years on end, they just keep right on buying that same wrong size. To see if you fall into this group, try this simple measuring test.

- Take the measurement, in inches, of your rib cage, just under your breasts. If that number is odd, add five; if it's even, add four. That number is your bra size.

- Then take the measurement, in inches, around your bustline at the fullest point.

- If the difference between the first measurement and the second is five inches, you are an A cup.

- If it's six, you are a B.

- A seven-inch difference means you are a C cup.

- And eight inches means you need a D cup.

problem stems from the fact that so few people who sell bras really know the product. The only way you get to know a product is by actually being hands-on and fitting it on people—not by just standing behind a counter and directing people to a rack. It's really a shame that you're left on your own in most lingerie departments. That's where the need for smaller lingerie stores comes in. If you have a problem finding bras that fit in some vast department store lingerie area, you should try a smaller store where you hope there will be somebody who can help get you into a comfortable, attractive, well-fitting bra.

Now this will merely give you a starting point, but bear in mind that different styles of bras can fit differently (so never buy one without trying it on first), your breast size changes throughout the month, and your breast size can change radically if you've gained or lost a lot of weight, are pregnant, or just finished nursing. Anytime your body has gone through a significant change it's a good idea to measure yourself again and reevaluate your correct bra size. Or better yet, go to a store where someone knowledgeable can not only measure you properly but give you suggestions on the right styles and types of bras for your size and figure.

So many of us give little thought to our underwear, but the right bra really is a necessity before you buy clothes. I've had to send women away to get proper bras before I could fit clothes on them. It's really true that what you wear underneath has a genuine effect on what you wear over it. For instance, I often see women wearing these lacy, fussy bras under thin cotton T-shirts, and it looks absolutely horrible. And then there are the women who have such an obsession with push-up bras that they put them under everything—even tight, high-necked tops—with little thought to what kind of look they're creating. A woman may love the way she looks in the bra, but she doesn't stop to notice that when she pulls her top on over it she's got a lump over each breast because the push-up is forcing her to spill over the top of the bra. If she had on a low-cut top, that cleavage would look very voluptuous, but when those extra lumps are trapped under a shirt, it just looks ridiculous.

Unfortunately, there really is no way to tell how a bra will look under your clothes until you actually try it on under your clothes. That's why I always bring a thin, fitted sweater or a tight T-shirt into the dressing room when a customer is trying on bras. It's a very easy, quick—and virtually foolproof—way of finding out how the bra really looks. It doesn't cost you a nickel (and it can save you countless dollars because you avoid buying lots of costly mistakes that end up banished to the back of the underwear drawer). It's really a very good trick because a bra can fit perfectly and look good on its own yet still look absolutely terrible once you get that sweater on over it. I can't tell you the number of women who've fallen in love with a bra only to find it looks awful under their clothes. I'd even recommend bringing a couple of different tops—something silky and clingy, something slightly sheer, something rather form-fitting—with you and trying each of them over every bra you put on. This may sound like a hassle, but it really will save you trouble in the long run. And besides, I really think bra shopping should be its own trip. Don't try to squeeze it in when you are buying lots of other things. Make it an outing unto itself.

If you need to buy a bra to wear under something specific—like an evening dress—that you don't want to lug with you to the store, check to see that the bras are returnable before you buy anything. If so, you can take them home and try them under your dress to see which one works best. If the store won't accept any returns or exchanges on undergarments, then you might have to actually drag that dress to the store. And once

Bosom Buddies

No, it's not enough just to know what size you wear, because bras come in many shapes and styles. Here are the terms you'll need to toss around the lingerie department in order to get the right bra for your needs.

- Padded: These generally have cups that are padded (either a thin or thick layer) evenly all over. Best for: anyone who wants to increase her overall bust size significantly. Also good to wear under tight tops if you want to make sure your nipples don't show through.

- Push-up: Like the Wonderbra, most push-ups are underwire bras with extra pads that slip in for more boost. Be sure to try these on both with and without the extra pads for the right fit. Best for: creating cleavage.

- Demi cup: Rather than a full cup that encloses the entire breast, these underwire bras have half cups, wide-set straps, and work by pushing in from the sides. Best for: enhancing A and B cups who have trouble filling out a full cup.

you are completely satisfied that you've bought the right bras, you really should wash them before wearing them. That's a habit that's carried over from my childhood, but, as usual, my mother was right about it. Hand wash them or put them in a little mesh bag on gentle cycle in the machine, and line dry (believe me, they'll last a lot longer if you care for them properly). After a couple of washings, the bra will contour to your body better. It takes the points down and softens up the fabric so that it's also more comfortable against your skin. Another trick for looking less pointy is to pick a bra that has cups with seams that are sewn on an angle (as opposed to straight across the breasts). The angled seam shows less through your clothes and helps the cups contour better to your body.

THE BOTTOM HALF

Although fitting a bra is certainly a much more exact science than fitting a pair of panties, dressing your bottom half

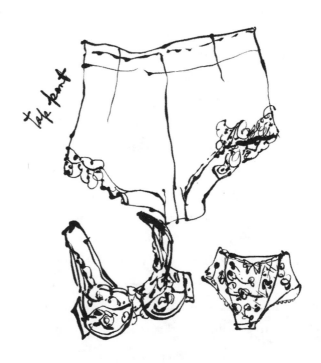

is not without its problems. First of all, a panty has to be comfortable—meaning it doesn't bind you at the top and doesn't creep inward from the sides. But I think many women would even go so far as to forsake comfort if they could be guaranteed relief from fashion's biggest don't: the dreaded panty lines. Those Underalls ads from a million years ago really touched a national nerve. Not a day goes by without a customer (or most likely, several customers) getting a panicked look on her face when she puts on something new and catches a glimpse of her rear view. The next question out of her mouth is, What can I wear under this that won't show?

Well, I think we owe an awful lot to the strippers, since we're all now wearing the G-strings they've been strutting around in for years! Are pasties next in the lingerie department? Seriously, though, the thong is the only way to go if you want to wear anything super tight (like leggings) or super clingy (like a thin jersey skirt or a bias-cut silk dress). And every day I have women asking me, Are thongs comfortable? The only answer I can give them is, You be the judge. Nothing is more of a personal preference issue than the thong. Some women love them. Some hate them and fidget all day when they have one on. Some like them to have just a thin strip in the back, some like it wider. I do find that people seem to have less trouble with them if they are worn under stockings because everything stays in place better. Or maybe you're just already so uncomfortable from your panty hose you hardly notice the difference!

Lingerie

- **Underwire:** Any bra constructed with curved wires beneath the breasts. Best for: support.

- **Soft cup:** Any bra constructed without an underwire. They need to fit perfectly or you will have a baggy cup. Best for: A and B cups who don't want a lot of support.

- **Molded cup:** These are designed so that the fabric holds to its own shape, and if it's a sturdy fabric you will get good support and more separation. Best for: C and D cups.

- **Seamless:** Cups that are completely smooth with no seams at all. Best for: wearing under tight tops.

- **Front close:** Bras that hook in between the breasts rather than at the back don't offer as much support because the back hook is more adjustable. Best for: smaller busts or anyone who wants a more natural look.

- **Racer back:** The straps come together in the back in the style of a racing bathing suit. Best for: wearing under sleeveless clothes that are cut out at the shoulders.

→

- **Strapless:** Any bra without shoulder straps. There are also long-line strapless bras (which come down to the waist), which are more comfortable for larger bust sizes. Best for: wearing under any strapless or thin-strapped dress.

- **Wrap around:** The shoulder straps adjust so you can elongate them, and then they wrap around and hook in front at the waist. Best for: accommodating low-backed dresses and tops.

But if you aren't planning to wear clothes that would necessitate a thong, you should simply look for a comfortable panty that won't cause lines or bulges under ordinary fabrics and styles. Ones that come all the way up to the waist eliminate the problem of having two lines to contend with—one at the waistband of your panty hose and another a few inches below it where your bikini panties hit. For the smoothest look, try panties in fabrics like stretch lace, fine cotton, or a sleek microfiber. And here's a great way to test a pair of panties (especially if you can't try them on): Take a pair and lay them flat, front side up on a table. If the leg holes sit in flat Vs, chances are the pair will give you a line (and quite possibly will also ride up on you). If, on the other hand, the leg seams are rounded and curl slightly up and in, that means they will form around the natural shape of your behind and be much less likely to present problems.

Another option exists for those who can't be bothered to put on two separate pieces of underwear each morning. It's the bodysuit—a full-length blend of bra and panty. The big advantage is that you eliminate the lines that would normally result from the band at the bottom of your bra and the one from the waistband of your panties. These are, however, a lot harder to fit properly. How many of us are so perfectly proportioned that our bust, hips, and waist all fall into place? And since bodysuits are sold according to bra size, you have to try on the one that is sized for your bust and hope the rest of you follows suit. Your best bet is to look for a bodysuit that's made from very stretchy fabric, that way you will have a little bit more leeway in the tummy and hips. But I don't care how stretchy that fabric is, if you are taller than about five feet, nine inches, you are going to have an awfully tough time finding a bodysuit that's cut long enough for your torso.

The other bra and/or panty alternatives are tap pants and camisoles. Tap pants are more like little shorts—usually made from a loose-fitting, flowing material—than they are like panties (in fact, they shouldn't really substitute for panties but be worn in addition). Many of my customers buy them to wear like little half slips under short skirts. And camisoles are the perfect solution for the small-busted woman who doesn't want to wear a bra, or you can wear them over your bra. I wear them like undershirts to keep warm under my clothes. They're the perfect solution for a sweater that's a little too itchy, and depending on the style of the camisole, you can even let it poke out the top of a low-buttoned blouse, cardigan, or jacket.

A Panty Briefing

What you wear is your business, but you should know what your options are when it comes to underthings.

- **Briefs:** These are your basic, full-cut, high at the waist, low at the leg underpants.

- **French cut:** Briefs that are cut very high on the leg.

- **Bikinis:** These have a waistband that generally hits somewhere around hip level.

- **String bikinis:** A skimpier version of the bikini—basically two triangles (front and back) connected across the hip with a narrow band of elastic.

- **Thongs:** Also known as a G-string, the thong is cut down to just a strip of fabric at the back.

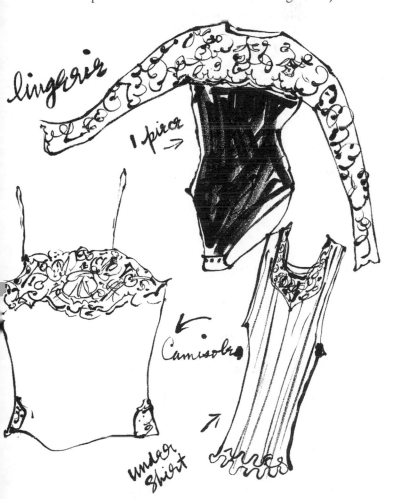

lingerie

1 piece →

Camisole

undershirt

Part 3

NIPS, TUCKS, AND PADDING

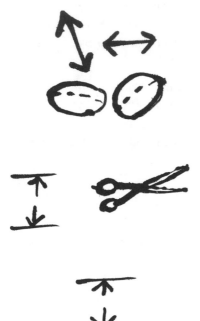

*T*he word *girdle* is so antiquated now that I doubt if many young women even really know what one is. Back in the old days, a girdle was absolutely de rigueur—no one would be caught dead going out of the house without wearing one. But the advent of panty hose changed all that, and eventually even the most proper ladies tossed out their painful old girdles. The slip has also gone the way of the girdle. Anytime someone (usually an older woman) comes into my dressing room wearing one, I'm shocked. But I do notice that they find it cumbersome while they labor to try on clothes, and very often they discard the slip midway through. Sometimes, as soon as they see that they don't need all those layers under their clothes, they free themselves of the slip for good. I see them roll it up and stick it in their handbag or simply leave it behind.

Yet somehow, in the midst of all this freedom and people walking around girdle-less, slip-less, bra-less, and sometimes even panty-less, a little revolution began in the form of new high-tech Lycra body shapers. I think it all started with the Hipslip, that neat little half-slip with a built-in panty that was designed to suck in the tummy and mold the buttocks and thighs into a more svelte line. It makes sense: Clothes keep getting more and more form fitting, and our aging bodies often can't keep pace. But I see young, thin, size four women buying these things as well because they just give you that extra smoothness under a slim-fitting dress. The all-in-one types are especially good because they eliminate all of those lumps and bumps that aren't you but that are caused by layers of underwear and stockings, etc.

There is one problem with bodysuits, however. Sometimes

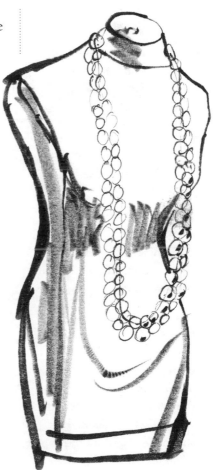

Control Yourself

Yes, bodysuits and control panties are wonderful. But, no, they aren't miracle workers. Here's a little reality check on what sort of results you can expect.

• They will help you to squeeze into a dress that is slightly too small, but they won't take you from a size ten to a size six.

• You can tame the jiggle in your backside, but you cannot (without diet and exercise or surgery) create "buns of steel."

• They cannot take the place of time spent on the Stairmaster.

• Even the tightest waist cincher probably won't give you a nineteen-inch waist. (Then again, why would you even want one?)

• The seams make the difference between shaping and merely flattening. For example: A bike short with a seam that runs straight up the middle of your backside will give you a rounded shape. One without the seam (or with side seams) may merely flatten you out.

they're not so easy to maneuver in. I love the feeling of the light Lycra bodysuit. You really do feel so much slimmer. And I think I would wear it more often—maybe even every day—except that a few times when I've had it on, I've gotten myself stuck in the ladies' room. There I am in my evening dress and I can't pull the

154

elastic together to fasten the bottom. And who do you yell for when that happens? It's not like a broken zipper for heaven's sake.

The great thing about these control panties and so on is that, if you want to wear one, there's probably one out there made to do exactly what you want it to. A size six woman who works out all the time will slip into one before putting on a tight skirt to smooth out that tiny bit of jiggle she can't seem to get rid of at the gym, while the heavier woman will wear one to hold her in all over and make her feel thinner and look firmer under all of her clothes. And as the concept becomes more and more popular, manufacturers are creating shapers that are targeted to specific "trouble spots." You can get a high-waisted brief with a control panel for the tummy, a panty designed to sculpt your rear, long-line knickers to tame jiggly thighs, and even longer ones that hide bulgy knees. Whichever you choose, the net effect is the same: You end up with a sleek, lump-free, line-free silhouette under even your most form-fitting clothes.

Chapter 8

CLOTHES — AN OWNER'S MANUAL

Part 1

CLEAN UP YOUR ROOM!

**The words spoken between Betty and me are costume-talk, but she always knows precisely what I'm saying and we go directly to work. Occassionally we stop for water or tea . . . but it's the rapture of her expertise that I cherish.
—Ann Roth, costume designer**

You've been hearing that line since childhood, and you've probably also been despairing over your lack of storage space for just as many years. The truth is, very few of us are lucky enough to have all the room we need for stockpiling our clothes, shoes, accessories, and plain old junk. Why else would an entire business of closet organizers have come into being? Now if you can afford to have a closet professional come and rebuild and reorganize your closet for you, then you might as well skip this chapter. For those of you who want or need to figure it out on your own, read on.

Cleaning out your closet is undoubtedly one of the most hateful (and hated) chores around—worse than laundry and scrubbing the bathroom combined. But if you truly want to get and stay organized, you have to commit to regular closet

cleanings. And when I say cleaning, I mean it. I mean that every six months or so you take every single thing out of the closet (maybe deciding to get rid of a few items), and wash the shelves and vacuum the closet floor before putting everything back in. You'll be amazed at what you find in there—especially if you haven't seen your closet empty since the day you first moved into your home. Not only will there be dust bunnies galore, but you will probably also unearth some items of clothing you haven't seen in ages. Take a good look at what you find, and remember that not all of it needs to end up back in the closet. Cleanup time is also a prime opportunity for sorting through—and perhaps tossing out—all those clothes that have been trapped in the dark recesses of your closet. So many packed closets are really just graveyards of "mistakes" no one wants to get rid of. I've said it before: Bite the bullet and give away those things you haven't worn in years and probably never will wear again.

Now that your closet is spotless and the number of things that need to be put back in it has been drastically reduced, it's

empty closet

time to rethink your organizational techniques to find the best way of using the available space. First, take a good look at the setup of the closet itself. Is there room to add a second bar, perhaps higher or lower than the current one? Is there shelf space above the bar? If there are simple modifications that can be made (like adding a second bar or some additional shelves), now might be a good time to hit the hardware store or find a carpenter who can do the remodeling inexpensively. And while you are shopping, pick up several storage boxes that are small enough to fit on the shelf over the clothes bar but large enough to hold bulky items. Closet stores and catalogs like Hold Everything have made a big business selling clever storage gizmos, but you can easily find cheaper options at discount stores, hardware stores, and in catalogs like Lillian Vernon.

Now take all of your out-of-season gear and put it aside. If it's spring, take your sweaters, turtlenecks, gloves, scarves, and hats (plus a few mothballs). If you're heading into fall, put aside your bathing suits, T-shirts, and shorts. Now put all of these out-of-season things into your new storage boxes—don't forget to label them!—and then stack them up high where they are out of your way until the seasons change and you need to drag them down again.

Another key to using all of your available space wisely— and to keeping your stored clothes looking good—is learning how to fold. I think folding is one of the great lost arts. A good way to practice is to take a new folded men's dress shirt (one you just bought or one that's still freshly folded from the dry cleaner) and use that as your model. Take another shirt and try to fold it along the same lines, with the same neatly squared corners and uniformity. It takes a little patience—sort of like learning to knot a bow tie. After a few tries you will start to get the hang of it, and you'll see how shirts and sweaters that are folded neatly and uniformly are more stackable and take up less space in your storage boxes and on the shelves. I find that most people don't use their closet shelf space to the best advantage. Even if the shelf is placed high over the bar, if the usable space goes up from there to the ceiling, use it. Get a step ladder, climb up, and stack those storage boxes up to the ceiling. If you only put things in them that you don't need for several months, then it's really no inconvenience having them so inaccessible.

Besides the storage boxes, you should make a few other space-saving investments to get your closet truly organized. There are hangers designed to latch on to each other, and they are ideal for hanging blouses, since you can hang six to eight shirts, all neatly nested together, using the space of just one hanger. Similar nesting hangers are also available for pants and skirts. Now, at the risk of sounding like Joan Crawford in *Mommie Dearest*, please, no more wire hangers. They really are damaging to your clothes—garments simply don't hold their shapes properly on them, and they break down the shoulders of jackets and knits. Multiple hangers are essential if you only have one bar in your closet, but if you have room to hang a second bar lower, you can use that one to hold shorter items like skirts and shirts, while the longer hanging space can be used for dresses, coats, and pants. For storing evening dresses and other pieces worn only occasionally, pick up a couple of large garment bags designed to hang in the closet. You can shove these to the back of the closet so that they are out of sight and take up a minimal amount of valuable space, but the clothes inside will still be well preserved.

The real idea behind all of this organization (besides saving your clothes from an untimely demise) is to help *you* be more efficient every morning when you get dressed. Let's face it: We tend to wear only what is right in front of us and easy to grab when we open the closet. If you have to search for it (or if

organization is 90%

you find it and it's a wrinkled mess), chances are you'll never wear it. So, by tucking all of your out-of-season clothes neatly away and putting the current stuff front and center, where it's readily accessible, you will probably end up actually wearing more of your wardrobe. And the bonus is that once you accomplish this major organizational overhaul, maintaining it is easy. All it takes is the few seconds to hang up or fold everything neatly and put it back where it came from.

So now everything is back in the closet and beautifully arranged—except for your shoes. Shoes have a way of ending up in a huge, messy heap on the closet floor, pairs tend to lose each other, and if the closet is dirty enough they are even covered in dust by the time you unearth a matched set. The easiest, cheapest, and perhaps most obvious way to keep your shoes neat and organized is to store them in their original boxes (you can attach a Polaroid of the pair to the outside of the box to eliminate guesswork about the contents). That way they are covered and protected, and you can stack them either on the floor of the closet or on an overhead shelf (also a good place to store out-of-season shoes). Along the same lines, but slightly more expensive, are plastic boxes that you can buy at any closet store and maybe some places like K mart or Wal-Mart. Although using these requires the time to transfer all of your shoes from their original boxes, the benefit is that they are clear, so you can store your shoes yet still see them all—which can save a lot of fumbling around the closet in the morning. For those who prefer to have uncovered shoes all laid out before them, the best solution is a stackable shoe rack, which can easily grow as your shoe collection increases.

If you want to get really fancy with your shoes, there are

a variety of hanging gadgets and shoe doors that can attach either to the closet doors or to the hanging bar, allowing you to get the shoes off the floor entirely. I have built-in shoe doors affixed to my closet doors that have been there for thirty-five years. A carpenter can install them, and even though it is probably the most expensive option, I think they are invaluable. They are basically an extra door, the width of a shoe, hinged onto the inside of the closet door. The shoes hang by their heels from the bars which run across. If you have extra hanging space, you might want to try one of the cloth shoe bags that loop over the closet bar and then have individual compartments to hold several pairs of shoes. Again, the most important things are organization and accessibility, so think about what will work best for you before you go out and revamp your entire closet space just to accommodate some shoes.

Now comes a trickier part: What do we do with all of the non-hangables? I'm talking about the piles of panty hose, socks, belts, bags, lingerie, jewelry, and scarves. Okay, the belts and bags are easily dealt with by some hooks, or even nails, affixed to the closet walls (or a multihook belt hanger), but organizing the rest of those items will require emptying out and reorganizing the dresser drawers. Let's start with your panty hose and sock drawer. I find that usually messy problem solvable in a very simple way: I roll my hose and socks up, bagel style, and line them up in the drawer that way. You can see them easily, and best of all, when you reach for one, only one comes out. If you have a lot of scarves, the best way to deal with them is to fold them neatly and line them up, standing on end, and then use a jewelry box or a couple of bagel-rolled pairs of socks to hold them in place (like bookends). If you pack things

Betty once thanked me for wanting to help her hang things up, which I did out of guilt for the volume of things I had tried on to find one suitable piece. I figured that if I tried on ten things to find one, I'd better help hang them up. Betty wouldn't let me, but gave me credit for knowing how. In all honesty, I'm too content to step over my things at home, but at Betty's house, I mind my manners.
—Jane Pauley, anchor, *Dateline NBC*

in like that it will be as if the whole drawer is held together with invisible "walls" that divide and keep everything in its proper place.

The underwear drawer is another spot where everyone seems to just toss it all in and hope for the best. But once again, folding is the key to keeping everything neat. Someone really should teach a class on how to fold—it's like origami! Fold the panties in thirds and store them in piles according to style and color—that way, even as supplies run low, you'll still know without rummaging whether or not you have any clean black thongs or a nude, high-waisted panty. Same thing with bras. If there is still room, fold your nightgowns or sleepwear T-shirts and stack them in the same drawer. In one of these drawers—the underwear or the sock drawer—you might want to leave some space for piling up jewelry. I like to keep good jewelry in its original box to protect it from getting lost amid all the costume stuff. If you get drawer dividers (even like those you keep in the kitchen for silverware) you can stash all your junk jewelry in a somewhat organized fashion—organized enough at least to find what you want as you dash out the door to work. I know a woman who took a strip of fabric and hung it on the wall with all of her earrings tacked onto it—a true bit of earring sculpture.

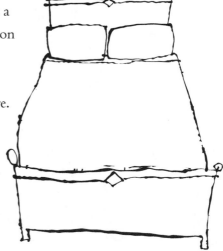

And since, no matter how organized you are, there are always those odd-shaped items that don't seem to fit anywhere, baskets and other sorts of decorative compartments are a storage Mecca. You can stuff them with everything from magazines to laundry to gym clothes—just about anything that has nowhere else to go. I don't know if this basket trend started on some remote island or in a college dorm, but it is a very worthwhile addition to storage solutions. The only method of stowing stuff that I absolutely abhor is under-the-bed storage. Better to store out-of-season clothes at the cleaners than to stuff them under the mattress. There is something about that out-of-sight, out-of-mind aspect of it all that makes me think you will never again find what's under there.

Part

2

OUT, OUT DAMN SPOT

*E*veryone treats laundry like the plague. And often, in the rush to get this odious chore out of the way, delicate clothes get ruined, stained clothes go untreated, and darks and lights get all wrapped up together. Now I'm not going to give you a complete lesson in how to wash your clothes, but I will share a few secrets I've learned over the years for spot cleaning and hand-washing things yourself with great care. But no matter how many tips I give, I'm afraid to tell you to try this yourself, because I know that most people are so inept at cleaning that the minute they try, it's ruination time. I've seen customers come running in with a gravy stain the size of a pinhead, but the water ring around it (from their attempt to get rid of the stain) is the size of a silver dollar. In other words, if you aren't completely comfortable, march yourself and the stained garment straight off to the dry cleaners and leave it in the hands of a professional. I'm pretty

good at this, but I too have made rings that don't come out.

And once those rings are there, you're out of business.

But after all these warnings, you can still spot-clean a

stain if you are very careful. Take an old bath towel or wash rag

and cut it up into small pieces. Take one piece and place it on

the underside of the garment to be cleaned, then put a drop (if

you use too much you get all suds and no action) of Ivory

liquid or some other dishwashing liquid on another piece of

toweling and rub it gently onto the stain. Be *very* gentle. You

don't want to ever scrub roughly, abusing the cloth or the spot.

If the spot is going to lift, you'll notice it start to lighten

almost immediately. Then rinse the spot you've cleaned with

cool water and pat, pat, pat to dry without getting a ring. If

you do end up taking your stained clothes straight to the

cleaners, do yourself a favor and be sure to point out the spot and tell the cleaner what caused the stain. If you throw stained things in with all of your other dirty clothes and roll the whole thing up in a wad to drop off, you'll get the garment back in the same condition. And you end up paying for that stain—twice.

One easy bit of spot cleaning that anyone can do is scrubbing off the dreaded "ring around the collar" from white shirts. I don't wear makeup on my neck, but every time I wear a white shirt the oils from my skin still make a mark on my collar and cuffs. When I take the shirt off at night, I just take a nailbrush and some Ivory liquid and scrub. It takes two minutes, and you don't have to do it every single time, but a big residue does build up if you don't do it occasionally. And it really is the only way to get them clean. The laundry won't get it and neither will the dry cleaner.

Look at the care label on almost any sweater and you'll see the same three words: Dry clean only. Well, I know the cleaning establishment won't like this one bit, but your sweaters really will get cleaner and last longer if you hand-wash them instead of sending them off to the dry cleaner. The key is to use a very light dose of liquid soap detergent (or even baby shampoo) in cold water. I say a light dose because if you use too much soap, your sweaters will be awash in suds that will be very hard to get rid of and you'll end up rinsing for hours. Let the sweaters sit in the sink until they are completely soaked through with water and then rinse two or three times until all traces of soap and suds are gone. Then when you take the sweater out of the water, roll it up in a bath towel and squeeze the water out gently. Do *not* wring your sweaters out because you'll ruin their shape and leave hard-to-get-rid-of wrinkles. Unroll the sweater and lay it flat on a dry towel, smoothing it out and positioning it into its original shape. Turn the sweater over periodically while it dries, smoothing it into shape each time. When it's dry, shake it out and, if you are truly brave, finish it off with a cool iron. The sweater will have regained its fluffiness and will feel cleaner and smell better than if you just pulled the plastic off of it from the dry cleaner. I promise this is a safe way to clean all of your sweaters—cotton, wool, silk, angora, cashmere, whatever—and they really will feel nicer and hold up better in the long run.

I learned a really neat trick just the other day, that has to do with care—not cleaning. So many clothes now are being made from that wonderfully stretchy and clingy jersey material, but the problem is that after several wearings you start to get bags at the knees, elbows, and so on. All you have to do is take the stretched-out garment and pop it into the dryer (don't wash it first, these fabrics do need to go to the dry cleaners). Turn the dryer on the delicate cycle and let it spin for a few minutes. When you take the garment out, all those baggy parts will have shrunk back into place.

As long as I'm giving you lessons on caring for all of your clothes, let's not forget about your shoes. I'm always amazed by how many women—many of whom spend a good deal of money on their shoes—will walk around in scuffed, worn-out looking, unpolished shoes. Don't be intimidated by the nearly all-male environment at the shoe shine shop. There is no reason why women shouldn't be able to enjoy the luxury of a professional shine just as men have been doing for so many years. Or, periodically treat yourself by taking all of your shoes to the shoe repair shop and picking them up a few hours later looking shined and good as new. But really, doing it yourself is not such a big job either, and your shoes really will take on new life. All you need is polish, a chamois cloth, and a good shoe brush. One night while you're watching television, simply line up all your shoes and work your way through them. And don't

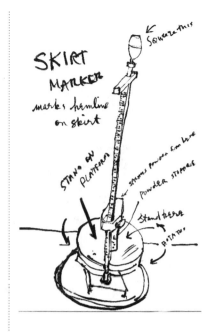

forget about your leather bags: Empty them out completely (pat them down to catch all the things you can't even believe are hiding at the bottom) and give them a little polishing and buffing. It not only makes them look better immediately, but it will also keep the leather more supple in the long run.

Suede shoes—which, I have to say, I consider to be one of the ultimate luxuries—are, unfortunately, more delicate than leather and there is no secret formula for reviving them. I keep a wire suede brush handy (you can buy one at any shoe repair shop) and brush my suede shoes against the nap every morning before I put them on. This not only cleans out some of the dirt, but it will also help bring back the rich color of the suede. There are also a variety of cleaning and waterproofing sprays available, but the bottom line is that suede is really too delicate to ever be completely waterproof. Suede shoes just aren't meant to withstand repeated soakings, so the biggest favor you can do for your suede shoes is to keep them out of the rain as much as possible. If you

do get caught in a downpour in suede shoes (or leather ones, for that matter), don't just take them off your feet dripping wet and stow them in their box in the closet. They'll never dry properly and God knows what will happen to their shape. Instead, take a few pieces of tissue paper (or even a few sheets of paper towel) and stuff the toes. That will help absorb the moisture and help the shoes to maintain their proper shape while they dry out.

I grew up in an era of patent leather, and now that it has made its way back into

cleaning shoes w. wonder bread

fashion I often find myself giving customers lessons on how to clean and care for their shiny new patent leather shoes and handbags. Every single one of them looks at me in amazement when I tell them that the best tool for cleaning patent leather is a slice of white bread (yes, I mean like from a loaf of Wonder bread). It truly does work to wipe off smudge marks and restore the shine. If you have white patent leather (or any other light color), you can try a little bit of nail polish remover to get rid of black scuff marks, and then clean the entire shoe with a bar of Ivory soap and wipe it down with a clean washcloth.

Besides the regular cleaning you do on your own, it is a good idea to take shoes to the shoemaker about once a year (depending on how much walking you do) for a sprucing up. New soles and heels can be put on for about $30, and as long as the upper portion of the shoe is still in good shape, you'll come out with a pair of shoes that is literally as good as new.

When you go on these periodic cleaning binges, don't forget about all of your jewelry—it gets dirty too. Sterling silver jewelry especially needs to be cleaned frequently because the oils in your skin blacken it over time. You can use the same paste or liquid polish you use on your good silverware, warming the jewelry in hot water, then cleaning and rinsing it thoroughly with cool water. For periodic maintenance (or for things, like a silver buckle on a leather belt, that you don't want to immerse in water), pick up a silver cloth at any hardware store. Gold jewelry doesn't tarnish as easily, but it will look amazingly bright and shiny if you treat it to an occasional cleaning and wipe it dry with an old, soft washcloth. And while you're at it, remember to drop your pearl or beaded necklaces off at the jewelers to be restrung every year or so. Not only will the necklace look better (newer, cleaner) afterward, but the maintenance investment will serve as a good precaution against breakage.

Part

3

PACKING IT IN

Traveling used to be an awfully genteel experience. I remember when I was a little girl, you wouldn't go on a train or a plane or even a bus without your gloves on. You always had to have a special traveling outfit. And the luggage! We had little hand trunks with hangers inside, huge hard-sided suitcases, and everything was extremely heavy. But then again, you always had a porter meeting you at the other end to carry it to the car. Now, you really are on your own. Most of the time you can't even get a cart to push your bags around the airport. It's no wonder everyone has started pulling around those little black cases with wheels. It's either that or duffel bags slung over every shoulder.

Since whatever bag you choose to carry is going to accompany you on many trips—probably over the course of many years—you want to be sure you choose the best sort of bag for your sort of traveling. Your suitcase really has to match

your personality, the way you pack, and the way you travel.

When you go shopping for a suitcase, keep all of these things

in mind. Do you hate to check your bag? Then make sure the

bag you buy is compact enough to qualify as a carry-on. Do

you like to roll your clothes up rather than folding them? Then

you should consider a duffel instead of a traditional suitcase.

Are you able to haul a heavy bag over your shoulder? If not,

check out the wide array of wheeled cases. The latest models

can be pushed or pulled to get through the airport without

breaking your back.

But no matter what you pack *in*, the bottom line is that

less is definitely better. I have to admit that I myself have to

fight the urge to be a very heavy packer. I always think there

won't be a store where I can buy that extra pair of panty hose

or whatever if I need them. But the less encumbered you are the better your trip will be. The trick is to minimize your options and think it all out very carefully beforehand. My bed becomes my table when I'm trying to pack. I lay it all out in front of me, then I take things away and put things back until I'm satisfied with my selections. I would never pull clothes straight from the closet and throw them into the bag. You really need to lay it out, count the days you'll be gone, and then plan accordingly.

Put the clothes together as outfits on the bed, starting with two outfits as your base and then building on alternatives from there. A basic pantsuit and a simple jersey dress make an ideal foundation, and work in almost any climate. Then you'll want to fill in with several alternatives—such as a fresh blouse or two, a sweater set, a camisole for the evening, a few T-shirts, a bodysuit, and another casual skirt or pair of pants to wear with the suit jacket. That way the outfits you create will work for both day and night and will carry you through several days of traveling. If you get to the point on your travels where you feel like you've been living in the same outfit, simply change the underneath part again—adding a fresh T-shirt or a new sweater.

Men are usually better packers than women because they don't take all of those "just in case" clothes. You know what I mean, because you probably do pack them. The sweater or coat for "just in case" it gets cold. Or the sexy dress for "just in case" you go to a nice restaurant for dinner. You have to try to rein in that "just in case" urge, because the trick to packing light is to pack things that all go together. You simply add on pieces in monotones. It might not be the most exciting way to dress, but it'll certainly make your load a lot lighter. And besides, who are you really seeing when you go on vacation? Is anyone going to notice if you don't put on an entirely new ensemble for dinner every night? Probably not. Unless you go to a resort or on a cruise, where you do get dressed up more and tend to see the same people every night. In that case you really do have to take more. There's no way of getting around it. But you can still follow the same principle of packing pieces that all intermingle and are all in varying shades of the same tone. You really shouldn't have anything that doesn't go with everything else.

Look at it spread out on your bed before it goes into the suitcase. Is there a foreign object there that really sticks out? If so, it should probably go back in the closet and you should substitute something more basic that you know you'll wear on more than one occasion during the course of your trip.

Now that you know what you want to pack, it's just a

...Plan accordingly

matter of knowing how to do it. I believe that the real trick to packing is to put everything in plastic. I watch my daughter when she arrives at my house—she's an expert packer—and everything that comes out of her suitcase is on a hanger, encased in plastic, because it all came straight from the cleaners. I swear I think she intentionally gets everything cleaned right before she leaves just so it will all be in plastic bags and ready to go. Well, I don't rely on the dry cleaners; I put it all in plastic myself. I bring the plastic dry cleaning bags home from the store (and I can't tell you how many rolls of them I'm always sending off to my customers who travel a lot), but you can also just save the ones you get every time you do go to the cleaners. Take them off your clothes and stuff them in an empty suitcase so that you'll have them handy next time you need to pack.

I start by twisting two wire hangers together. Now, generally, I hate wire hangers, but I find if you put two together it's almost as thick and sturdy as using a wooden hanger (but takes up much less space in your bag). If you want to be really meticulous about it, wrap a few pieces of tissue paper around the bottom of the hangers to give your clothes a little padding and prevent anything you hang over the rung from ending up with a crease. Then take the hangers and start layering clothes onto them as if you were dressing a body. I'll hang all of my pants over the bottom rung, I'll bend up the ends and hook my skirts (by those little loops sewn into the waistband) over that, then pull T-shirts over that, blouses over that, and top it all off with a jacket. Once you've loaded as much as you can on the hangers (without causing them to sag), you pull the plastic cover down over the whole thing. It becomes a protective layer for the clothes, and it really is the only thing that wrinkle-proofs them.

Once you've got it all on the hanger and covered in plastic, you simply fold the whole thing in half and put it in your suitcase, or if you're using a garment bag, just hang it up. I've gone away for three weeks with all of my clothes layered onto three sets of hangers. It's a fabulous way to pack.

The plastic also helps keep your folded clothes in better shape. I compartmentalize my duffel bag: one end for shirts and sweaters, the other end for T-shirts and maybe shorts in the summer. Then the aisle in between gets filled up with lingerie, panty hose, and sleepwear. And I know it may sound a little over the top, but I do put all of these things in their own plastic bags—like the kind you would use to store vegetables. But instead of corn and green beans, you've got socks and underwear!

Everyone always hates unpacking when they arrive somewhere—and yet I *refuse* to live out of a suitcase—so I had to figure out a solution to this chore. You'd be amazed at how easy it is to empty out your suitcase if you pack this way. Just open your dresser drawers and *bim, bam, boom,* toss in your vegetable bags. No fishing around for that lost pair of tights or the black bra because everything's right in the plastic baggie where it belongs. I honestly think you can actually fit more in your suitcase this way too.

Speaking of room, if you have enough—and foresee doing some shopping during the course of your trip—I highly recommend packing an empty, squashable duffel inside your suitcase. I have a duffel that folds up to nothing that I always take along as an extra. I've even brought home pottery that way. I take a couple of big, soft sweaters and use them as you would bubble wrap, completely cushioning the pottery. I haven't broken anything yet. The key is to pack so that you use every nook and cranny. I don't lose any space when I pack. Your things will stand up better for the long haul, and, of course, you'll also be able to fit a lot more in a bag than if you just packed in little piles.

I have a way of sticking things in things. Take a purse, for example: I would never pack an empty purse because it loses its shape. If you took a soft, quilted Chanel-like bag and stuck it in your suitcase empty, you'd have a dented, concave bag when

you arrived. And you can't stuff enough tissue paper in it to really keep it puffed up. So I always take a few sheets of tissue and stuff that into the bottom of the purse, then fill up the rest of it with my junk jewelry—like big plastic bangles and clunky chains. I do the same thing with my shoes: I'll fill up the toes with pairs of stockings or even a few pairs of earrings. Try it. You'll be amazed at how much more you suddenly fit into the same suitcase you've always carried.

Years ago, the really diligent packers wrapped and stuffed things so full of tissue that you could hardly find the clothes amid all the fluff. When I went on my honeymoon—we're talking a lot of years ago—a woman actually came to the apartment and packed all of my clothing in stand-up steamer trunks, and in those days you took *everything*, including several changes of evening clothes. She stuffed each outfit to the gills. When I arrived in Hawaii I was *loaded* with tissue paper. I swear there must have been enough to fill the whole room, and what was I going to do with it? God knows my clothes weren't going home that way!

If you travel with your clothes in a hanging bag, I've got another great trick for you that I learned at the store. This is how we send out clothes when we put together a wardrobe for a movie or television show. Usually there are tons of items, but the customers don't want them arriving in dozens of bags, so we came up with a way to fit the same number of outfits in drastically fewer hanging bags. Go to the dime store and pick up a bunch of those inexpensive plastic hangers (the kind with the little hole at the top, right where the hook of the hanger swivels). Now layer all of your clothes on a few of these hangers and hook each of the hangers together through the hole at the top. Start by hanging your longest item (like a coat) on the first hanger and work your way down to the shortest items (a blouse or miniskirt). You can keep hooking them together until you fill the entire length of the garment bag—but the whole thing is still only one-hanger thick and therefore *much* easier to fold in half and carry. You can also take a couple of pairs of shoes and line them up along the bottom of the bag to fill out the frame. When I said I like to use every inch of space, I wasn't kidding.

You know what they say about the best-laid plans, well unfortunately, the same holds true for the best-packed bags. Yes, what I'm trying to say is that—despite all the plastic, the tissue, the hangers, and the careful packing—you probably will still have a few wrinkles to contend with when you arrive at your destination. My best advice is to gather up whatever is looking a little crinkled and head straight to the bathroom. Hang everything up, turn the shower on as hot as it'll go, close the bathroom door, and pray. Pray that the water will be hot enough and that you don't flood the bathroom (I've nearly been kicked out of a few hotels for trying this trick in places with leaky plumbing). Once in a while, go in and give the clothes a good shake, and turn them around to see if the wrinkles are hanging out. This method will work on most fabrics, but don't expect to get miraculous results on heavy cottons or linen. But that's really something to think about before you pack: Try to pick fabrics that generally don't wrinkle so readily and that hang out easily when they do. Silk is great, and stretchy nylon fabrics, velvet, and lightweight wool crepes will all revive quickly in a steamy bathroom.

I'm always surprised when sweaters wrinkle; somehow you never think of them wrinkling, but they do. There have been times when I pull a sweater out of the suitcase, and it looks like my face looks when I get up in the morning! Packing them individually in plastic bags should help prevent this, but you can also hang them to get them back in shape. Generally, I advise against hanging sweaters because it wreaks havoc with the shoulders and the shape, but if you stick them in the steam, the wrinkles should vanish long before the hanger has had enough time to create points in the shoulders. If you have the extra room in your suitcase, I'd highly recommend toting along a handheld steamer. They're marvelous, and can work out most wrinkles in about five minutes. I bet I've had mine for over thirty years, and it's still going strong. And best of all, if you use a steamer, you can stop worrying about flooding the bathroom!

Chapter 9

TAKING
THE STORE
BY STORM

Part

1

GOOD HELP IS HARD TO FIND

Given our rushed and chaotic world, working with Solutions (as the name implies) provides that brief but necessary respite when order is restored, priorities recognized, the stars align, and optimism prevails. All because Betty has produced the perfect outfit.

—Patsy Tarr, publisher, *Dance Ink*

Sometimes I think my customers fear coming to see me the same way they fear going to the doctor. Granted, you've got to strip down to next to nothing for both of us, but I'd like to think I'm nowhere near as intimidating as a doctor. As I see it, the real similarity is that, just as you need to find a doctor whose opinions you trust and who makes you feel comfortable, you need to find someone in your favorite store who can do the same. It can be a personal shopper, a sales associate, or the owner or manager of the store (in the case of a small boutique), but the key is to establish a relationship with some knowledgeable, helpful, pleasant person who can help eliminate some of the hassles that are unavoidable when you try to go it alone. Now I'm not suggesting that this person become your Svengali—the way some of my more insecure customers turn to me before making any move is rather disconcerting. But finding someone and developing a relationship, a little one-on-one, will make your life a little bit easier.

Believe it or not, I think stores are actually starting to get more and more service-oriented. Bergdorf Goodman (and several other upscale department stores) has people known as "greeters" posted at every entrance who are there not only to welcome you but to help guide you in the right direction through the maze of the store. These people are generally very eager to help, plus they have been educated about every area of the store—from couture to T-shirts. I think another reason service is on the rise is that more and more people seem to be making a career out of being a sales associate or a personal shopper or store manager. And if you can find and gravitate toward one of these professionals, then more credit to you.

> The first time I met Betty, I was at Bergdorf Goodman trying on a very beautiful black lace dress. She walked by and started a serious conversation with my two young children, who were on the floor rolling around in their snowsuits, bored. Anybody who could get my daughters' attention certainly got mine. On that day, the four of us began a friendship that's lasted to this day. And for well over twenty years my daughters and I have been asking, "Betty, what do you think?"
> —Jo Carole Lauder

Stepping into these big stores can be intimidating. It even happens to me, though I've worked in a store for twenty years, when I go to other places. Some of these stores have salespeople who seem to be purposely rude. They think they can still judge a book by its cover, but if everyone's walking around in jeans and T-shirts, how do they know what is in everyone's wallets? I was shopping with a friend recently and she said, "Who do you have to know to buy a pair of shoes around here?" No one wanted to wait on us. Now this nonchalance about selling is almost worse than being pounced upon the minute you walk in the door.

The truth is, it's tough business trying to find the right person to steer you through the buying process. I can't make you any guarantees, but I can at least give you a few guidelines and a couple of quick tests that will make it easier for you to accurately assess the sales help you encounter. The first step, as you scan the store for a salesperson is to find someone willing to make eye contact with you. Anyone who is too indifferent to meet your "I need help" look—someone who is on the phone, chatting with his or her friends, or staring into space chewing gum—should be avoided like the plague. Please don't waste your time trying to convince this person to help you. Just move on and keep looking until you find someone else.

A good quick test, which will show you how experienced and knowledgeable the sales associate is, is to ask about sizes. I can look at almost any woman (sometimes even with her coat still on) and tell what size she is. Now I'm no mind reader: This is a skill that has come out of years and years of fitting clothes on bodies and knowing who goes into what. But test the knowledge of the person waiting on you by holding up a pair of pants you'd like to try on and asking, "Do you think this size eight will fit me?" If the answer is yes, but you are usually a size ten or twelve, then you should question her judgment. Either the person has a very astute eye, sized you up properly, and knew that those particular pants run big (in which case you've found a gem) or she has no clue and is just trying to make a sale. Often, if the store is out of your true size, the salesperson will try to sell you what is available, offer to alter it, attempt to convince you that that's the way it is supposed to fit, or simply talk you into something that's not really right. Don't let a salesperson waste your time by making you try on millions of garments to find the correct size and style for your body. If the salesperson doesn't pass the size test, just say thank you and move on. Finding someone else, or even grabbing several sizes yourself and heading to the nearest dressing room, will ultimately take less of your time than working with an uneducated or uninterested salesperson.

You should also be wary of a salesperson who starts to kill you with all kinds of accolades. The words, "Oh, it's *you!*" should put you immediately on the defensive. When someone goes on and on about how lovely you look in something, feel free to question her as to why she's saying it. Say to her, "I'm actually not sure it fits right" or "I'm not sure this is really the right color for me." You have every right to question, because after all, she's not paying for it, is she? And she's not the one who has to live with it hanging—unworn—in her closet.

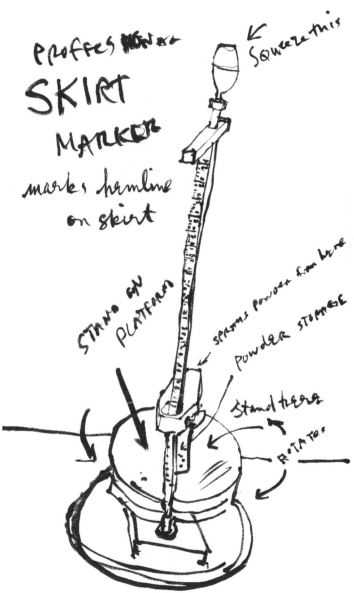

Even once you've found someone to help you, gathered several items, and been escorted to a dressing room, you are still not in the clear. Haven't we all had the frustrating experience of being trapped in the dressing room with the wrong size pants, hollering through the door for some assistance? There is nothing more frustrating, because unless your salesperson happens along (or is conscientious enough to come back on her own to check on your progress), you are forced to get entirely dressed again to go back out to scour the racks for the correct size. There is no foolproof way to ensure your salesperson sticks around, but it can't hurt—as you close the door behind you—to ask her to come back in a few minutes because you think you might need to try the next size up.

When (or should I say if?) you finally do find a sales associate who is helpful, knowledgeable, and seems to understand what you were looking for, he or she can be invaluable—and not just while you are at the store. Every single sales associate at Bergdorf Goodman keeps a client book that includes the addresses, phone numbers, preferred credit cards, sizes, favorite designers, colors, and styles, and so on, of all of their customers. So not only can they speed you on your way when you are at the store shopping, but they can help you plan your shopping trips better by letting you know in advance when something you wanted is going on sale or when a new shipment of sweaters you might like is coming in. The stores are beginning to realize that service like this benefits the stores as well as the customer, because one satisfied customer can bring in an entire family—as well as friends—of new customers.

I think one of the biggest mistakes women make is to assume that most store services can be enjoyed only by the rich. Not so! I don't care if you're shopping at Bergdorf Goodman or Sears, you shouldn't be treated any differently based on how much you are—or might be—spending. In most stores, consulting a personal shopper is absolutely free, and the service is not contingent upon emptying your wallet and leaving with heaps of expensive items. Everyone is equally entitled to work with a personal shopper or to request a call from a salesperson when an item goes on sale. Just as you could go wade through the entire coat department on your own, try on a hundred coats, not find one you like, and leave empty-handed, you could call a personal shopper, have her pull a few selections in your size, help you try them on, and you can *still* leave empty-handed.

Regardless of whether you've consulted with someone or tried to shop alone, the other trap we all fall into is intimidation. Truly the best advice I can give you is: Never feel compelled to buy anything. There's nothing wrong, if you're scared out of your rocker (by the salesperson, the store, or the prices), with saying, "Thanks, I'll be back," and walking straight for the door. You must not be intimidated into buying. Just because someone has brought you things to the dressing room to try on does not mean you have to buy them. You are not indebted to this salesperson no matter how helpful she was. Even if she had to scour the stockroom or undress a mannequin in order to find you the jacket you wanted in the right size, you still don't have to buy if you put it on and don't absolutely *love* it. And you also don't have to sneak out of the store. You should be especially firm if you are trying on something that you feel is a little bit too expensive for your purse. Never get badgered or embarrassed into buying anything you can't afford. Are you trying to impress the salesperson that you have enough to buy whatever you want? Of course not. So don't get bullied into acting that way. You'll only get home, regret the purchase, and then feel like you have to slink back to the store to return it—often making up some

Tips for Sizing Up a Salesperson

- Someone who greets you at the door or approaches you as soon as you walk into the department is eager to please.

- If you are walking around with clothing in your hand and the salesperson doesn't offer to get you a dressing room, he or she is not going to be very helpful once you're trapped behind the dressing room door with the wrong size pants.

- Beware of the salesperson who is too busy chatting on the phone or huddling behind the counter with her friends to even glance in your direction.

- Someone who checks on you periodically in the dressing room—but isn't annoyingly intrusive—is someone worth seeking out again.

- If you hear the salesperson giving the same compliments to you and every other customer, feel free to question his or her objectivity.

excuse or another about why you decided you didn't like it after all.

When you do decide to make a purchase, don't forget to take advantage of the other big service most department stores—and even many smaller shops—offer. And that is free or well-priced alterations. I can't tell you how many times customers have bought dresses that needed to be shortened, slimmed, and into the customer's closet all on the same day. Higher end stores are usually better at making these sorts of accommodations, but if you're not in that much of a hurry, you can usually get whatever alterations your garments need within a few days or a week. And how much easier (it saves time too) it is to have it pinned right in the dressing room before you take it off than to buy it, take it to another tailor, and try it on again for pinning?

Everything fits so differently today—one size ten is huge in the waist, another is tight in the shoulders—that I truly don't see how anyone can just take something off the rack and expect it to fit. I look at a lot of people walking around and I have to say that I think most of them don't wear their clothes to the best advantage. They are far too willing to just wear them as is, even if they are too big under the arm or the shoulder is too broad or the length is a little off. Men are much better about this because they are used to having their suits tailored—the pants cuffed, the jacket sleeves adjusted. So why do women (who, on average, spend a lot more on clothing than men) allow themselves to make do with somewhat ill-fitting clothes? I think that many times women are too intimidated to ask for alterations, but you absolutely must—you'll be amazed at how much better you can look in your clothes.

Whenever you buy anything, be sure to ask the salesperson if they have anyone on staff who does alterations. I think you'll be surprised at how many stores do provide this service. Most big department stores do, as well as most small boutiques and even certain chain stores like Banana Republic. And don't be intimidated by the prospect of a fitting—let the tailor give you his or her advice about what needs to be done to the garment. Sometimes it's a simple matter of a hem (but what a difference the right length skirt can make), but you'd be surprised how much better a suit can often look if the skirt is trimmed down and the jacket's shoulders narrowed. The difference is that suddenly you have a suit that looks like it was made for you. Your clothes look more expensive when they are tailored properly, and that's not to say that expensive clothes necessarily fit perfectly right off the rack. Expensive clothes often look better because the women who buy them understand the value of getting them tailored to fit perfectly.

Granted, tailoring your clothes can be very costly—even if you do use the store's own services. But I promise you it is worth the expense because it will add value to your clothes and will make you happy every time you put them on. In my opinion, you'd be better off buying one less item of clothing than you had planned on buying at the start of each season, and then use the extra money to get everything you purchased tailored to fit you like a glove.

A friend of mine in New York recently had a shopping experience that proved to me that you really can get good service at any price level. Sometimes all you need to do is ask. He went to a big, established store that has branches all over the country looking for a tuxedo. He found the jacket right away, but the New York store didn't have any matching pants in his size. First the salesperson called stores all over the country to no avail, and then he gave the customer the phone numbers of all of their outlet stores in the East. One call led to another

until a pair was finally located in Vermont and airmailed, on approval, to see if they matched the jacket. A few days later, the manager of the New York store where the jacket was bought called to follow up and see if my friend had managed to piece together his tuxedo. Now *that's* service, from both the store and the outlet (where you'd think no one would be inclined to help you with anything).

And apparently this story is not entirely unique. I have heard of women who fall in love with a certain designer jacket or dress when they try it on, but who don't feel comfortable purchasing it at full price, so they have the salesperson write down the style number and then call the designer's outlet stores in search of the piece. It seems that many of these outlets have surprisingly good service (perhaps they are trained to keep up the designer's high-end reputation). Not only will they ship items to you if you order them by phone, but some will even keep an eye out for requested items and call interested customers when the item arrives. Which brings me to another good point: At an outlet or any store that offers it, put your name on the mailing list. That way you will always be informed—normally in advance of the general public—of upcoming sales and the arrival of new merchandise.

A BARGAIN BY ANY OTHER NAME

I don't care whether you're on a tight budget or have money to burn, every woman I know loves to find something great on the sales rack with the price so drastically reduced that she feels like the store is practically giving it away. And I agree that there can be a tremendous sense of pride and accomplishment when you do come away from the store with a Calvin Klein cashmere dress for less than the price of a cotton jumper from the Gap. The problem, however, arises when you get so caught up in the pursuit of the almighty bargain that you forget to take into account little things like your size, the colors you like (and don't like), what you already own, and what styles suit your figure. I call it "sale brain." What happens is that the minute you catch a whiff of those markdowns (the same thing happens inside outlet stores or at designer sample sales), you lose all reason and shopping savvy.

> Betty handles planeloads of Texas heiresses and soap opera costume designers with great skill, leaving everyone happy and well dressed. As an old client, and also an old friend, I depend on Betty for a cup of coffee, good advice on my wardrobe, and personal service— whether it's getting a ride in the rain in a Bergdorf delivery truck with a tulle party dress or a recommendation on what to wear for an unexpected television appearance the next morning.
> —Betsy Cronkite

Things that you would not have even glanced at when they were full price suddenly become utterly irresistible at 50 percent off.

There are women who only buy on sale—women who shop every day on their lunch hour, stalking their favorite items of clothing as they make their way from full price down to the third markdown. To be truly successful at this, you have to be a shopper extraordinaire. Anyone who is able to ferret out the good stuff from what is normally a rack full of junk is someone I would call a very savvy shopper. These are probably the same women who can walk into a junk sale and come out with a priceless antique for five dollars.

But if you are going to shop the sales you have to keep repeating to yourself, Do I need this? Do I really look good in this? Because the bottom line is, most people make hideous mistakes when they get bargain-crazed. And the truth is, most stores now send their truly good merchandise off to the outlet stores rather than putting it on the sale racks. You are much better off at the outlets, where the merchandise is displayed in a more attractive way, you have a greater selection to choose from, and you are more likely to find your size.

I know you probably don't want to hear this, but I have to say that there are very few situations in which it really makes any sense to purchase something on sale that you wouldn't have also wanted to buy while it was still full price. If you've been coveting something that was way out of your budget, kept an eye on it, watched it go on sale, and then went back and bought it, that's great. That's the Great American Dream—at least as far as shopping is concerned. But here's a cautionary tale from the dark side of sale shopping: Let's say that you peruse the sale rack at the end of the season and come across a Ralph Lauren silk shirt—and you've always just *loved* Ralph Lauren but couldn't afford any of it—that's been marked down 75 percent. A great find, right? Well, not necessarily. Let's say you've really been looking for a red silk shirt to go with a suit you own, and this one happens to be in a rather bold shade of green instead. If you can afford to buy it and still have money left to go in search of the red one you really need, then, by all means, get it. But don't be seduced into buying it if you don't like the color, have nothing to wear it with, or won't ever wear it. In other words, don't buy it *just* because it's Ralph Lauren and happens to be affordable. My point is that anything you buy but don't love enough to want to wear all the time is certainly no bargain, regardless of how low the price tag goes.

Another big problem that is often the result of buying a so-called bargain is that people end up with a piece of clothing that doesn't fit and can't really be fixed. Blinded by slashed price tags and visions of all the money you're saving, you manage to convince yourself that this size twelve jacket can be easily (and inexpensively) made to fit your size eight body. Or—worse yet—that you really will lose the five pounds that will enable you to squeeze your size twelve hips into size ten trousers (or that you will find a tailor who can let them out). My motto is: If it can't be fixed, don't buy it. And a lot of these clothes really can't be fixed. You might as well take a pair of scissors and cut

The Five Caveats of Sale Shopping

Here's what to keep in mind so that *sale* doesn't become a four-letter word in your wardrobe's vocabulary.

- Do use end-of-season sales to stock up on basic, untrendy items like T-shirts, sweaters, classic coats, and casual, weekend-type gear.

- If the season isn't over yet, shop the sales as a way of picking up on a trend without spending a fortune (this goes for shoes as well).

- An item that's stained or damaged beyond repair is no bargain.

- Be careful about shopping the sale rack for your wardrobe's core investment pieces. These are things you will (hopefully) wear a lot, and you don't want to feel like you settled for the wrong color or a slightly different style than what you really wanted.

- Don't buy anything unless you truly love it (this holds true at full-price, on sale, or at the outlet store).

the garment up and throw it away—that's what a waste of money it is.

Ideally, there is a tailor or alterations person on staff at the store who can tell you what can and cannot be done to a piece of clothing before you go and make the costly mistake of buying a nonreturnable, nonfixable sale item. But since that is not always the case, you need to learn to look for yourself (and look with a realistic eye) at how the garment is made, where it doesn't fit, and what can reasonably be done to alter it. Generally, people put on something that's too small and assume the seams can be let out. Increasingly, as manufacturers try every trick to save fabric, there is nothing left in the seams to let out. You have to learn to look and feel for the seams, and to hold the garment up to the light and see if there is extra fabric at the seams. And even if there is, some fabrics—especially velvet, satin, and certain silks—cannot be let out because the original stitching leaves an indelible mark. Taking things in can also be a problem if you aren't realistic about what can actually be done. Trying to go down more than a size is virtually impossible because it's really like making a whole new pattern, and it can be very difficult to get the armholes right and reduce the shoulders properly, and yet still keep everything in proportion.

Very often, what people think can be remade is absolutely ludicrous. Either it can't be done at all (and the garment winds up as closet dressing) or the necessary alterations are so costly that suddenly this piece of clothing you thought was such a bargain ends up costing more than buying another whole outfit at full price. You would be better off shopping until you find something else rather than taking a risk. There really is only so much that can be done to an article of clothing. After all, it's not a living, breathing animal—it's just a piece of fabric.

WHICH WAY IS UP?

Part

3

Chances are that if you shop mainly in big department stores you feel just as overwhelmed and confused each and every time you step through the revolving door. It could be the same store you've been going to since your mother took you there in your stroller or you could be in a foreign store in a foreign city, but that disoriented feeling remains the same. It descends on you the minute you emerge into the bright lights, dizzying colors, and heady scents. (Why is it that you're always forced to fight your way through the perfume spritzers and cosmetic counters before you can get anywhere?) Now if you are in your long-standing favorite store, you are probably adept enough to navigate your way through this maze and emerge virtually unscathed at the elevators where you can whisk yourself straight up to your favorite department.

If, on the other hand, you've just entered the great

> When I first met Betty, all I had were problems! The store intimidated me, I had no idea of how to dress, and I was terrified of spending any money at all. Now, thanks to Betty, I have overcome my fear of the most elegant store in the world, learned the meaning of a good suit, and learned—with her guidance—how to spend wisely and well.
> —Bridget Potter, senior executive vice president of entertainment, NBC, New York

199

unknown, you should make a beeline for the nearest store directory to get an idea of which floors hold the types of things you're looking for. And then, rather than just hopping on an elevator, ride the escalator up and up and up—it'll give you a much better vantage point for checking out the lay of the land. In fact, that's why stores started using escalators instead of just elevators in the first place: They force customers to see the whole store rather than just the one department they're seeking. Think of riding the escalator as window shopping—except that you do it from the inside and you can hop off the escalator at any floor that catches your eye.

Better still, take a little time out and actually wander through the store as you would through a museum. Poke your head into every corner, every department, and check out all of the "exhibits." Touch, feel, look around, and get familiar with what the store has to offer you. Don't worry if you get lost; that's all part of the game. The stores want you to get lost. They want you to end up in an unexpected department you never would have wandered into otherwise. You can do the same thing at the mall, stopping into all of the small specialty stores. Don't discount any of them until you've gone in and had a look around. Chances are you'll find a lot of similarity in all of these stores or in the various areas of the department store. That's what you can get rid of right away. If you know that two stores or two departments within a store have similar selections, then cross one off your list. And that is precisely why this little exercise will actually save you time in the long run. Because if you do your homework and cruise the store with your eyes open (but your wallet firmly shut), the next time you go you'll know exactly where to head and where to avoid.

You really do need to keep a tight rein on your pocketbook so that you don't start picking up pieces of this and that as you cruise through the store. You may even want to leave your credit cards safely stashed away at home if you feel you're not to be trusted. Then just say to yourself, I'm not out to buy anything today. I'm not looking for anything specific. I'm just here to learn what's being offered and make mental notes to myself. Because if you like what the store has to offer, you *will* be back—maybe the very next day. The difference is that on your next trip you will at least have *some* sense of where you want to go and what you want to buy.

Now I realize that no matter how much I try to convince you that taking a tour of the store will ultimately be a time-saver, some of you busy types out there are saying, Hey, I just want to buy bras, or a pair of sandals, or a red cardigan, why do I have to wander the whole place first? So fine, walk in and walk up to the store directory, but be prepared for more confusion. If "women's shoes" are listed on three different floors, where will you go? Or sometimes the directories give such chic names to their departments that even after reading them you're not sure where to find new bras. More and more stores are providing pamphlet-size directories (look for them near the elevator or escalators) that are often more helpful and explain in greater detail where things can be found. Plus, you can carry the directory around with you while you

shop in case you have a sudden urge to find the coat department.

The hardest part about writing this book is realizing that I can't be there to take each one of you by the hand and lead you around the store as I do with my customers. You, unlike my customers, will have to take what I've tried to give you and then fly solo. In the end, all I can really do is try to instill some bravery in you. Get you to open your eyes and look at yourself, the store, the clothes, the salespeople, and the whole shopping experience with a little objectivity (and always, a little humor). Also to urge you not to simply follow the fashion herd. I've always said that if we truly do become a nation of sheep—of nothing but clones—that will be my cue to close up shop. Nobody should need help figuring out how to dress just like everyone else. It's dressing like an individual that requires some skill, some effort, and at the very least, a little thought.

I think women are all way too critical of themselves because they are so busy looking at other women—their bodies, their hair, their clothes. And we're so busy trying to cover up, conceal, and disguise. I've always known all my life that that's not what style is about. It's how you hold your head that makes you attractive. It is—I'll say it one last time—a matter of confidence. It's because of this insecurity that I so often hear the lament, I have *nothing* to wear. This problem normally has very little to do with a lack of money, a lack of time, or even a lack of clothes (women with the most overflowing closets still claim to have nothing to wear). This is about a lack of imagination, a lack of self-confidence, and the boring habit of always trying to play it safe.

You may think that you bought all the wrong things, that nothing you own goes together, or that it's all just pieces without a single complete outfit. These are all valid dilemmas, but chances are, you are either not really suffering from these problems or can solve them without even making a trip to the store. The real problem is most likely boredom—you wear the same three suits mixed with the same three shirts during the week, and the same jeans, khakis, and sweaters every weekend because those things have become like your security blanket. Very often you can get over this feeling simply by redoing your closet. Bring some things forward and move those old standbys to the rear for a while. Take that red suit that makes you think, Why did I ever buy this? every time you open your closet, and try it on with a fresh eye. Mix it up with different tops, bottoms, shoes, scarves, jewelry, or belts. If nothing else, throw the jacket on over jeans and a black sweater.

And then there's the woman who never seems to buy clothes in outfits—instead she just picks up one piece at a time whenever and whatever strikes her fancy. Someone should go along with her and slap her wrist. This is not the most logical way to go about building a coordinated, cohesive wardrobe. But, hopefully, somewhere in your mind, you bought all these pieces to go with *something*. I can't look into your closet and tell you what that is. Maybe you have one safety harbor, like the ubiquitous black sweater, so as you continually buy little skirts or pants or jackets, you know that you can take them home and put them all with that black sweater. If you have myriad pieces in the closet and still think you can't find anything to wear, you are just not rummaging enough.

Or maybe you are simply feeling dissatisfied, and you can't help but think that a new dress will make you feel better about life in general. Shopping often does satisfy some of that longing. And there's a sort of excitement attached to it—it's an almost naughty little thrill to go out and spend money, even if it's just $20 on a T-shirt. If you feel that way, then do go indulge yourself—buy something frivolous, trendy, basic, big or little. Very often when you do feel that way you wind up buying something you really love and will wear happily for a while—until it too eventually becomes part of the I-have-nothing-to-wear collection.

We're all shoppers, whether we like to admit it or not. And we all love clothes, and we all want to press our noses up against every store window we pass. Let's face it: You wouldn't have even picked up this book if the whole business didn't intrigue you at least a little bit. And that's what getting dressed is all about in the end. Sure, there's a practical side to clothing yourself, but what keeps it going—why stores stay in business and designers keep on designing—is that fashion is also a whole lot of fun.